SMALL BRAVE MOVES

SMALL BRAVE MOVES

LEARN WHY LITTLE ACTS OF BRAVERY ARE THE KEY TO LIFE-CHANGING LEADERSHIP

NICOLE M. BIANCHI

NDP

NEW DEGREE PRESS

COPYRIGHT © 2021 NICOLE M. BIANCHI

SMALL BRAVE MOVES

Learn Why Little Acts of Bravery Are the Key to Life-Changing Leadership

ISBN	978-1-63676-840-3	*Paperback*
	978-1-63730-202-6	*Kindle Ebook*
	978-1-63730-284-2	*Ebook*

To Dave,
the love of my life and best friend, who told me if this
book is any good, they will turn it into a movie.

To my Moe, Joe, and Nic,
for living life out loud with every small brave move
you make. You are my greatest masterpiece.

CONTENTS

Pay attention to your passions. They are the key to starting and finishing the book you are meant to write.

—BARBARA KINGSOLVER

INTRODUCTION

___

Let's roll!

Those were the last audible words of Todd Beamer, a passenger on the hijacked United Airlines Flight 93. Todd discussed their options with other passengers and flight attendants, and then they voted on a course of action. Ultimately, they decided to storm the cockpit and take over the plane. The group was planning to "jump on" the hijackers and fly the plane into the ground before the hijackers could follow through with their plan. First, Todd Beamer recited the Lord's Prayer and Psalm 23 and prompted others to join in. Then he said, "Are you ready? Okay. Let's roll."[1]

In a November 8, 2001 address from the World Congress Center in Atlanta, Georgia, George W. Bush invoked Beamer's words: "Some of our greatest moments have been acts of courage for which no one could have been prepared."[2]

___

1   George W. Bush, "Selected Speeches President George W. Bush 2001-2008," *The White House of George W. Bush,* National Archives and Records Administration.

2   Ibid.

This kind of dramatic act, like attacking hijackers, is what most people think of when they think of bravery.

Bravery with a capital B, and dramatic acts like this one, flow out of the practice of making brave choices in daily life and practicing small bravery.

When we think of bravery, we can't help but picture someone with a cape coming to save the day. We think of brave feats being performed by those in the military, firefighters, police officers, or doctors to resolve a crisis. The idea of being able to tap into this type of immeasurable courage is foreign to most of us, and these generalized beliefs about bravery—Bravery'isms—set unrealistic expectations. When the crisis comes, these heroes are ready to stand up and confront the situation. We simply can't relate since we aren't putting our lives on the line, nor are we superheroes.

What kind of bravery is there for the rest of us?

"When we think of bravery, we often think of heroism first. It's a grandiose idea made for people who, frankly, are not normal like the rest of us. It's unlikely (but possible) that you will do some brave act that miraculously gets filmed for TV and gets shared by millions of people on social media. And that's okay."

—TIM DENNING,
WRITER FOR CNBC AND BUSINESS INSIDER.[3]

---

3   Tim Denning, "Bravery Isn't Just about Being a Hero," *Medium* (blog), December 23, 2019.

Bravery isn't something you do once in a lifetime. It's something you have to practice, all of the time!

Let me tell you another story about these two kinds of bravery in my own life. In November of 2012, my mom shared her devastating diagnosis of cancer, which had already spread to the rest of her body. She had late stage IV lung cancer. There was no cure. Her doctor estimated she only had a few months to live.

I had to be strong and brave. I had to get in and engage with her and the team of doctors. I had to be able to listen, inquire, and challenge. I had to help her build a game plan with the most sustainable outcome. I couldn't acknowledge the possibility of losing my mom because we were too busy "fighting" the cancer. My mom turned a diagnosis of months into almost two years. But as cancer often does, it took over. The time had come to put down my armor, our *"We Will Fight"* mantra.

It finally hit me when we transitioned my mom to hospice care. The fight was over, and the true bravest moments were actually in front of me. I had to transition from warrior mode to being an end-of-life caregiver. For twenty-two days in hospice at her home, she would teach me about bravery. There's no single dramatic act when caring for someone who is terminally ill; there's just daily bravery required to keep moving forward, which is what bravery requires of most people—small brave moves every day.

In the work I do with my clients, if I were to boil down the challenges that they face into one common element, it would be bravery or the lack of. Leadership development has been primarily focused on acquiring tools, like how to give feedback, how to tell a story, or how to give a better presentation. Those are important tools, but they're not enough. The framework or tool is useless if you aren't brave enough to have the conversation.

We have to shift the spotlight from just "leading" to becoming a braver version of our leadership selves! McKinsey & Company defines "leadership" as a set of behaviors leaders exercise to influence organizational members to achieve a higher alignment on the direction the organization is taking, to achieve a better execution of the strategy, and for the organization to continuously renew itself.[4]

Bravery is a skill. Leadership is an action. Without the skill, it can be difficult to take action. Brave leadership fundamentally involves being true to yourself and others, at the same time as honestly and transparently engaging with the external environment. It is about bravely leading from the inside out, an authentic and emotionally attuned engagement with self, and courageously letting the outside in. When pressures grow, difficulties arise. Multiple external drivers create complex challenges for organizations, and it is tempting for leaders to play it safe in the land of instruction, direction, and top-down strategy.

You can do the basics of leadership, but being the best leader requires bravery.

---

4   Simon London and Claudio Feser, "What Is Leadership: Moving beyond the C-Suite," February, 2019, in McKinsey Podcast, 30:57.

Bravery + Leadership creates a competitive advantage for leaders and it takes small brave moves to get there.

If you want to learn more about what it takes to live a life of small brave moves, bravery with a small b, then you are in the right place! This book is not designed to make you some iconic hero; you don't need a cape to be a braver leader. This book is designed to teach you the mindsets, behaviors, and habits that empower and enable you to be your bravest.

We all have a choice; we can just "lead" or we can lead as our bravest selves. What if we shifted the spotlight from just leading to being a braver leader?

About two years ago I was playing around with this notion and coined the phrase Bravership®. With Bravery + Leadership = Bravership, you can grow influence, accomplish more, and fear less.

We are going to explore how to build the skill of bravery: how to be bold with your boss, peers, and employees; practice and encourage open communication; and build a network that helps you make the brave choices. I don't promise once you master the book's content you will live every day with less fear or have it right every time. I do promise you will know research-supported strategies to build braver mindsets, behaviors, and habits.

The moves you make will compound significantly over time. You will need to do the hard work. You will need to get your butterflies in formation and practice these moves over and over. You will fail. You will get back up, and you will try again. No book or person (not even your loved ones) can make you excel, only you can.

PART I

BRAVERY + LEADERSHIP

1.

HOW WE GOT HERE

Me: "What is helping you be brave right now?"
Leader: "I don't think I am being that brave at all."

As I launched a new *Being Brave* series, a five-minute story featuring one leader and what is helping them be brave right now, I realized many leaders do not associate bravery with the work they do. Does that mean they are *not* being brave? Not at all. What I found was leaders expect to always have it right, always demonstrate executive presence, always have political correctness in all we do, and never let anyone see us sweat.

Speaking of sweating, let's say after reading a few articles about the benefits of dance, you decide to try it for yourself. At age forty, you sign up for an adult hip-hop class at a nearby dance studio. You put on some stretch pants and go. But when you get to the studio and see other adults walking in confidently like pros, their dance shoes slung over their shoulders, you begin to feel strange. Your heart rate speeds up, your palms grow sweaty, and you think, *why in the world did I ever think I could do this?*

This shaky feeling is vulnerability. It makes you want to turn around and go home, where you can escape the potential judgment of others and your own fear of the unfamiliar. According to Brené Brown, a professor and vulnerability researcher at the University of Houston, by pushing through those doors, you are doing something far more healthy and more transformative. In fact, "Vulnerability is the core, the heart, the center of meaningful human experiences," she says.[5]

In her book *Daring Greatly*, Brené Brown describes vulnerability as "uncertainty, risk, and emotional exposure. It's that unstable feeling we get when we step out of our comfort zone or do something that forces us to loosen control."[6] The book debunks myths about vulnerability, the most popular being vulnerability is a sign of weakness.

"What most of us fail to understand…is that vulnerability is also the cradle of the emotions and experiences that we crave," says Dr. Brown. "Vulnerability is the birthplace of love, belonging, joy, courage, empathy, and creativity."[7] So while going to that hip-hop class may feel uncomfortable, you're also opening yourself up to the opportunity to make new friends and learn a new, healthy habit. But if you run

---

5   Brené Brown, *Daring Greatly: How the Courage to Be Vulnerable Transforms the Way We Live, Love, Parent, and Lead* (New York: Penguin Random House, 2012), 12–14.
6   Ibid.
7   Ibid.

away the second those shaky feelings arise, you're just reinforcing the voice in your head that says, *I'm not good enough.*

Insecurity is present in all of us, and it's so strong that we often go out of our way to avoid situations that might make us feel fragile.

Over the holiday break in 2019, I did something I needed to do for the past few years—total knee replacement. I had been suffering from severe stage four osteoarthritis in both knees. Most days, it was painful just doing the basics, like walking.

I had taken on a semipermanent limp and dealt with daily pain. I wouldn't talk about it unless someone commented on my abnormal gait. Why? I was fine. It was fine. We were all just fine. Well… I wasn't fine. Only a few people knew I was undergoing this surgery.

I was busy doing all my final prep the day before surgery. I made sure the living room was set up for working and sleeping. I had one last thing to check off my list, to let the family know I didn't want any visitors outside of our immediate family at the hospital or at home after the surgery. Why? Because I knew I wasn't going to be feeling well, but mostly because I would be at my worst. Nobody should be a part of that.

My college-aged daughter, Moe, who was home on break and helping take care of me, quickly responded with:

"You spend every day seeing people at their most vulnerable and helping them become a better version of themselves. Now it's your turn."

She shot it to me straight. Her response was unexpected. But it was just what I needed to hear. She knew it and I knew it.

As a leader who advocates vulnerability as a strength, I was surprised to realize I had somehow bought into the notion I needed to be heroic, and any weakness diminishes my expertise or leadership. We must face the reality we are human. We have weaknesses, flaws, and faults. Yes, I am human with weaknesses, flaws, and faults.

Daniel Coyle talks about vulnerability and creating a sense of belonging in his book *The Culture Code*. He shares that vulnerability doesn't come after trust, but instead precedes it. Leaping into the unknown, when done alongside others, causes the solid ground of trust to materialize beneath our feet.[8]

I realized I had to embrace my vulnerabilities. I spent the following thirty days after surgery saying yes to offers for friends and family to stop over for a quick visit, drop a meal off, drive me to physical therapy, or just a hug when I was having a day filled with pain. When nobody was offering or asking, I practiced asking for help and leaning on my circle to deliver. And they did.

---

8   Daniel Coyle, *The Culture Code: The Secrets of Highly Successful Groups* (New York: Penguin Random House, 2018), 102–106.

The truth is, we have been taught to not be brave. On top of this, we allow fear to get in the way of being brave.

Fear comes in two different types:

Inherent Fears are intuitive and linked to our survival. They keep us alive.

Fears that hold us back are often learned fears.

Learned Fears usually develop over time due to psychosocial moments we experience when interacting with the world. If you don't gain the sense of trust in the world, then you'll resolve that through the lens of mistrust. These then become real fears based on our continued response to them. Learned fear is irrational and develops over time.[9]

The good news is these can be relearned.

In my work, I have found that leaders tend to struggle the most with three types of learned fears.

1. **Fear of not being perfect, not good enough**
Imposter syndrome was first coined by psychologists Clance and Imes in 1978. The imposter syndrome is a psychological pattern in which an individual doubts their accomplishments and has a persistent internalized fear of being exposed as

---

9   Nadia Kounang, "What Is the Science behind Fear?" (*CNN*: October 29, 2015).

a "fraud." Recent research shows it impacts both men and women equally.[10]

Who has reported experiencing it?

✓ Sheryl Sandberg, COO of Facebook, two-time best-selling author, ranked fifth out of fifty of the Most Powerful Women in Business by Fortune magazine;

✓ Tom Hanks, actor and filmmaker, the fifth highest grossing actor in North America;

✓ Michelle Obama, an American attorney and author who was the first lady, married to the forty-fourth president of the United States. Her influence remains high; in 2020, Obama topped Gallup's poll of the most admired woman in America for the third year running.[11]

Yours truly fights imposter syndrome. I deal with it regularly. I wanted to start my own company and talked off and on about it for several years. My fear of not being perfect or good enough was getting in the way. On top of my own negative self-talk, I was told by many leaders, "Oh, it will never work, you won't be successful."

Then one day my husband, Dave, asked me a few powerful questions:

---

10 Pauline Rose Clance and Suzanne Ament Imes, "The Imposter Phenomenon in High Achieving Women: Dynamics and Therapeutic Intervention," *Psychotherapy: Theory, Research & Practice* 15, no. 3 (1978): 241–247.

11 Stephanie Vozza, "It's Not Just You: These Super Successful People Suffer from Imposter Syndrome," *Fast Company*, August 16, 2017.

Him: "Why would you not start the business you keep talking about?"

Me: I sat there and shrugged my shoulders.

Him: "What's the worst that could happen?"

Me: "It fails. I don't get it right."

Him: "Could you go find another job?"

Me: "Oh gosh, yes, absolutely!"

Him: "So what's your next move?"

Me: "I am going to test it out, experiment, and see if I can do this."

That conversation was life-changing, and a tremendous weight was lifted. He knew I wasn't happy in my current role—more on that later. I knew I had a lot to learn and fast. Those powerful questions were life-changing nine years ago, and I have never looked back since.

THREE STRATEGIES TO DEAL WITH IMPOSTOR SYNDROME:

1. Focus on the facts.

List your achievements objectively. Allow yourself to take credit for your accomplishments. We tend to forget things not in the recent past.

2. Challenge limiting beliefs.

These are the stories we tell ourselves; they restrict the scope of how we see the world.

Limiting beliefs keep you from seeing all there is to the world.

Think about how the world looks when looking through the peephole in a door.

The scope is limited, and you can't see all there is to see.

If you were to look at life through that peephole twenty-four hours a day, seven days a week, how much of life would you miss?

Limiting beliefs act like that peephole.

Limiting beliefs keep you from seeing what is possible for yourself.

Maybe you think, "If I don't do everything and do it right, it won't happen." Doing the right thing should take precedence. Are you guilty of micromanaging? Do you watch every detail instead of the big picture?

Idea: Delegate, delegate, delegate, and empower yourself and those around you by giving them the opportunity to excel. Give yourself a break and others permission to make mistakes. Again, what is the big picture and are you losing sight of your goals because you are focusing on minutiae instead of the vision?

Maybe you think, "If there's something you don't like about yourself, it's better to hide it than express it or explore it." Do you hear yourself saying, "I can't. I'm too scared. I don't know enough. I don't have the right skills."?

Idea: Engage yourself productively in exercises that permit you to acknowledge your strengths and gain the confidence you need to become more secure. Identify and then conquer your fears. Having a conversation with our fears enables us to work through it. Give yourself permission to do what you need to do.

Have you seen the movie *Tag?* In particular, the scene where Bob Callahan, chief executive officer, is getting ready to walk into his big meeting with *The Wall Street Journal,* and you can see he is physically showing signs he is nervous. During his walk to the meeting, he says this out loud:

All right, Bob. You're the CEO of a Fortune 800 company.

You have commanded the respect of
coworkers and vendors alike

and that is why you're being interviewed by the big boys.

The Wall Street Journal.[12]

The scene above is a great example of affirmation statements. They help to remind us of our own accomplishments and how we got there by addressing our limiting beliefs. Examine your deep-seated beliefs about the criteria for success. Then look for facts or examples to test whether these criteria are valid, and how they might hold you back. Recognize the valuable perspective you've gained from personal hardships and don't let them hold you back.

3. Talk about it.
Lean on your circle. Share your feelings with trusted friends, colleagues, or an executive coach to put them in perspective

---

12   Tomsic, Jeff, director, Tag, *New Line Cinema,* 2018.

and help you reinforce the positive changes you are making. Then move on and move forward. Make one small brave move at a time.

I have a routine at the beginning of every speaking engagement or workshop. I do this to overcome the voices, the negative thoughts, and the imposter syndrome. On the outside, I may look like a pro who has it all together, but I am human. I experience much of the same, regardless of how many times I have done something. This is simple, I say these words out loud:

I know what I know.

I am glad you are here.

I am glad I am here.

I care about you.

Anyone can create their own words to say in their head to calm a fear. The words don't need to be fancy or a haiku. They just need to be a few words or a phrase you can own to find your focus and confidence. Doing this allows my butterflies to move into formation, which provides me the strength I need and lightens the intensity I have created for everything to be so perfect. It takes bravery to do the important work of leadership.

4. Fear of loss

Fear of loss can show up in many ways.

Fear of loss can stop us in our tracks from being brave.

A key principle that stood out in Lonny D. Meinecke's research during his dissertation was the finding that human beings are worried about losing things all of us are going to lose anyway. We are so worried about losing them, we would do absolutely anything to avoid losing them. But the "rational" fear of death doesn't make any sense. It's not as if we can avoid death. When we die, whatever we were all so worried about losing will no longer be ours to worry about. The irrational fear of loss is tough because someday, we will lose something we love very much. Someday we will lose everything we love.[13]

I feared losing my dad. One day, he was abruptly diagnosed with esophageal cancer. Our family had no notice, and we were ill-equipped for the journey. I was in my mid-twenties, recently married, and expecting my first child—his grandchild. All of us, including my dad, spent six months going through the motions and not saying what really needed to be said.

We all pretended it would be okay. But it wasn't okay. He passed away one morning as we all held him tight. He fought a brave battle against cancer. But we weren't brave enough to face the reality of what was happening.

---

13   Lonny D. Meinecke, "The Uncanny Fear of Loss," *Psychology Today*, April 14, 2018.

I was given another chance to practice. This time it was my mom, and it was lung cancer. Her journey was soon coming to an end. One afternoon she woke up and said, "We have to plan my funeral, grab your pen and paper."

We were running through the list:

- ☑ Church—check
- ☑ Pastor—check
- ☑ Songs/Bible verses—check
- ☑ Gathering after the funeral, the lame church luncheon—check
- ☑ Eulogy—she paused and said, "You have to do this, you are the only one who can." Her statement ended with a period, not a question mark. In my head I was thinking, *do you know how hard it is to even have this conversation with you? You and I are planning YOUR funeral. Mom, NOW THIS?* I paused and took a deep breath. After moments of silence, I asked an important question that had been weighing so heavily on my mind, but I hadn't been brave enough to ask yet.

"Okay, I will agree to do the eulogy, if you agree I can be there when you take your last breath."

She said, "Oh I don't think I have a say in that." I responded without hesitation, "Oh I think you do." I knew she didn't want to burden me or my brothers, and I wanted so badly to be there for her.

Just eight days later, I held her as she took her last breath. As promised, just days later I delivered a eulogy in honor of her that filled the room with laughter, tears, and pure celebration.

It took bravery to not just go through the motions of caring for her but to go much deeper. I could not let the fear of losing her stop me from being brave. During one of our final conversations, she told me she would always be with me as I held her hand. I asked, "How...?" She paused and said, "Look for butterflies...purple butterflies."

Not all losses are so extreme, yet they are all important to us. Another fear of loss is the fear of maybe losing our role or our job. One quarter of working Americans believe it is "very likely" or "fairly likely" they will lose their job or be laid off in the next twelve months, according to a Gallup poll. A 17 percentage-point swing in one year, from matching its lowest reading since 1975 to its highest, driven by the rapid impact of the coronavirus pandemic on the US economy.[14]

"We are the red bull in their mint julep," said our chief financial officer. Steve was referencing the merger of FirstComp with Markel Insurance Company. This was my last role on the inside before starting my business. I was the EVP of human resources and administrative services for FirstComp, on the front end of the merger leading people and culture.

What's the challenge? The acquiring company's human resources team proudly claimed to have systems and processes

---

14 "Record-High 25% of US Workers Say Job Loss Is Likely," Gallup, April 22, 2020.

from the '80s. What's the problem? I loved the '80s! This essentially meant the "merger" wasn't about us taking the best of both companies but instead unraveling everything we had built at FirstComp. One small example was moving from a sophisticated goal and performance management system to a word document with primitive performance information.

Fear of loss was making me hold such a tight grip. After about twelve months of traveling every other week to Richmond, Virginia and hitting my head against a brick wall, someone bravely said to me, "You are miserable to be around." *Wait, what?* I was too busy trying to drive change, unsuccessfully, that I didn't realize I had fallen out of sync with my role. Those words were a wake-up call for me and forced me to step back and scan every aspect of what was going on. At that moment, I realized I had a choice—fix my situation or move on.

THREE STRATEGIES TO DEAL WITH FEAR OF LOSS:
1. Make a list of your concerns.
Anxiety is powerful because it feels out of control and can send your thoughts on endless spirals. Ask yourself, "What am I scared of losing?" or "What is the worst that could happen?" These may seem like obvious questions, but I've learned it's all too easy to go through our days making choices without recognizing the underlying feelings motivating them. Whenever you have a choice to make, recognize the way you're motivated by the fear of losing something—whether it's comfort, security, control, money, companionship, or something else.

2. Ascertain if you're seeing the whole picture.

At one point in my life, I was working over sixty hours per week and traveling nonstop to hold onto a job I didn't even want. My logic was faulty. I believed it was best to stay with the sure thing because I wasn't ready to do something else. The reality was I needed the time and space to figure out that something else. If you're avoiding making a decision based on the fear of what you might lose, ask yourself if you're losing more by not doing what you really want to do.

3. Talk about it.

Lean on your circle. Share your fear with trusted friends, colleagues, or an executive coach to put them into perspective and help you process the changes you need to make. Then move on and move forward. Make just one small brave move.

4. Fear of change

We fear change because we lose control. No one likes feeling powerless.

Most people prefer the status quo. In fact, 62 percent of people either don't like to leave their comfort zone or do so only occasionally, according to Mark Murphy in his *Forbes* article about why people are terrified of change.[15]

I had been working on a case study looking at bravery from two perspectives.

---

15 Mark Murphy, "The Big Reason Why Some People Are Terrified of Change (While Others Love It)," *Forbes*, August 14, 2016.

Bravery in front of us: what is the bravest
thing I need to do right now?

Bravery behind us: what is the bravest
thing I did today or this week?

I had just walked in the door from a client trip in Florida,
anxious to try out my new questions. My son, Joe, had also
walked in after playing a high school lacrosse game. After a
big, sweaty hug, I asked him, "What's the bravest thing you
did today?" I thought I would test it out. He said, "Oh, Mom,
I played goalie at my lacrosse game; no one else wanted to
do it. I didn't either."

In the words of my sixteen-year-old, he said, "I didn't want
my nuts to get racked." *I was loving the pureness of his honesty.* He went on to say, "I did it for the team, so we could
have the best chance to compete. It turns out I am not a bad
goalie, and I learned so much from the goalie's point of view.
Mom, it's so much harder than it looks. The goalie may be
the biggest leader on the field."

In that moment, I remember feeling such an overwhelming
emotion of pride. Not just for him saying yes and trying
something new, but also pride in his self-awareness and connecting the moves he made to being brave.

Here is what we know: bravery is an acquired behavior! We
must practice brave moments to overcome our fears, just like
Joe did. When we are trying to be better at something, what
do we do? We practice.

Practicing small brave moves is the compound interest of self-improvement and growing as a leader. The same way money multiplies through compound interest, the effects of your small brave moves multiply as you repeat them. We sometimes dismiss small changes because they don't equal immediate big wins for us. Transformation takes time. Multiply your leadership success one small brave move at a time.

My husband, brothers, and friends will often say I am "lucky" about things that happen around me and to me. Actually, here is what happens. A swooning, "You are sooooooooooo lucky," followed by their heads shaking back and forth, which is embarrassing, and I always disagree. I use my preparation, attitude, and opportunity to see things others simply do not see, and then I act.

Darren Hardy shares in his book *The Compound Effect* his complete formula for getting lucky:

Preparation (personal growth) +

Attitude (belief/mindset) +

Opportunity (a good thing coming your way) +

Action (doing something about it) = **LUCK**

Preparation is constantly improving and developing yourself, which makes sense. He shares attitude is where luck evades most people. Seeing situations, conversations, and circumstances as fortuitous is simple. Opportunity isn't forced; it is a natural occurrence. Finally, it takes small brave moves to take action. The preparation, attitude, and opportunity can be in strong alignment, yet, are you willing to take the action?[16]

One of my best friends, Jodi, is the biggest Rick Springfield fan. She proposed a trip to Chicago to see Rick Springfield in concert and our friends said yes. When I say biggest fan, I mean printing and cutting out pictures of Rick singing and taping them inside her minivan for the road trip, creating a playlist filled with his top hits, and making matching shirts. Every karaoke evening includes "Jessie's Girl"! Her love for him is everywhere; there's no escaping it. We have all been friends since junior high, since the release of "Jessie's Girl," but don't do the math.

Screams echoed across the concert venue. Blackness seeped into every inch of the stadium, a promise for something big to come. The crowd was silent, aching with anticipation. Suddenly, the audience lit up in a sparkling sea of "Jessie's Girl" shirts as Rick took the stage. He started the show with an energy and staging most artists leave for their encore. A smaller venue, it was his Stripped Down Tour featuring solo performances with storytelling and a chance to get up close and personal with the man and his music!

I decided to run to the restroom after his fourth song in his playlist. I walked by a table with a beautiful, bright red electric guitar with a sign saying Meet & Greet. Meet Rick Springfield plus the autographed guitar—*opportunity*. I

---

16 Darren Hardy, *The Compound Effect: Jumpstart Your Income, Your Life, Your Success* (Boston: DaCapo Press, 2013), 31–32.

thought, *that is so cool.* I continued walking to the bathroom and immediately the wheels started to turn. I began "What if" scenarios in my head—*attitude.* I knew $400 would be a stretch for the girls to chip in as we were all still early in our careers, had young families, and we had the expense of an entire weekend in downtown Chicago.

Though it was early in my career, I had become very effective at building relationships, influencing, and negotiating at my job thanks to much practice in my roles at Conagra Foods, a Fortune 500 consumer packaged goods company—*preparation.* Walking back from the bathroom, I went up to the table, started a conversation with a young woman and asked about her and the package they were promoting. The deal was $400 and only one person could go back to meet Rick. She repeated the deal a few times and wasn't budging. My heart fell, *maybe I couldn't make this happen.* Then I said to myself, *keep going, you've got this.*

Next move, I launched into the story of my friend Jodi and her lifelong dream to meet Rick. She listened and began to smile as I shared how her childhood friends were here to support her love of him and his music. She began to laugh when I shared how she decorated her entire minivan with pictures of him singing for our viewing pleasure and regaled her with other stories of her Rick-fueled shenanigans. When I finally took a breath, she said,

"Let me see what I can do."

She returned shortly with Rick's lead guitarist, George Nastos. I knew the stakes were instantly much higher, my heart was racing, and I had to get my butterflies in formation quickly. It turned out he was filling multiple roles on this tour for Rick given the "solo" nature of much of Rick's singing. It was time for *action*. Introductions were made, and as he stood at 6'4" with his arms crossed, he immediately looked larger than life, looking less like the lead guitarist and more like the head of security for Rick Springfield.

He wanted to understand my ask. As I was sharing our story, I exuded energy and confidence, not just in the story but for the ask. I explained our situation, the travel to Chicago, and this once-in-a-lifetime opportunity to fulfill a lifelong dream for a friend. He was intimidatingly tall to my 5'6" frame. I took a deep breath and asked for the meet and greet for all of us at a reduced rate. He shook his head back and forth, not up and down. I relentlessly went on to convince him why the request must be granted.

It could have been my persuasive skills, or it could have been tour fatigue and dealing with yet another "Jessie's Girl," that led him to finally say *yes*! I don't know and I don't care. He instructed me to meet him at a specific location after the concert with my girls. I went back and could not stop smiling and singing my heart out. During the song before the concert ended, I spilled it! *"We are meeting Rick after the show! Oh, and we now own a guitar."* Jodi's reaction was memorable and etched into my heart forever. We were screaming like young girls and shed a few tears in disbelief.

Can we really just flippantly call this luck? No, we cannot. If you do, you don't yet understand the bravery and work that goes into creating opportunities and moments. How many of you would have just walked by saying it could never happen?

Because of the chance taken, the story shared, and the effort to build a relationship, we actually were invited back one more time to not just receive the guitar but to also see Rick. They could have just mailed us the guitar, but they didn't.

We allow fear, doubt, and the stories we tell ourselves to get in the way.

We play small, even when we have an opportunity to hit a home run.

It isn't always black and white. Always know there is gray. Never let an opportunity, which on the surface looks like one thing, define what could really happen.

To lead as our bravest selves, it takes small brave moves of mindsets, behaviors, and habits to manage the fears and lean into the vulnerability side of being a great leader.

It is a journey. It is your journey.

Why not learn to lead as your bravest self?

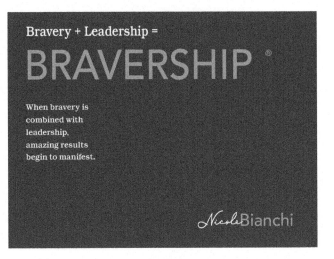

Bravery + Leadership =

BRAVERSHIP ®

When bravery is
combined with
leadership,
amazing results
begin to manifest.

Nicole Bianchi

2.

MINDSETS, BEHAVIORS, AND HABITS

"If people are going to tell you, 'you can't do it,' this should inspire you to do it that much more."

—NIC BIANCHI, FOUNDER OF BIANCHI CANDLE CO.

Over the course of the over twenty-five years working with leaders on bravery and leadership, I have found mindsets, behaviors, and habits can drive change, transformation, and progress. The important thing to note is we (you or I) can control each one of these things about ourselves. If we are not intentional, we can easily slide into a negative mindset, bad behaviors, and even worse habits. Ask yourself, *how do I want to be?* Then ask, *what mindsets, behaviors, and habits will help me get there?*

MINDSET

At its core, leadership mindset is defined by how we see ourselves in our professional roles and the stories we tell others about who we are. One of the most important, least understood, and most neglected elements in the evolution of a leader is mindset. Most of today's senior leaders grew up in a world driven by product innovation and operational efficiency. That environment shaped their experiences and career trajectories, determined what they valued and prioritized, and drove their decisions and behaviors. But that world has changed. Today's business environment is characterized by rapidly changing strategies, business-model innovation, and operational transformation.

Leaders trapped in yesterday's mindset often struggle to find their place and voice in this new business world. We find there are three mindset transitions that are consistently challenging:

The shift from functional to enterprise leader.

The shift from expert to manager or leader.

The shift from product innovator to business model innovator.

To successfully navigate these transitions, leaders must fundamentally change how they see themselves and their businesses. They must abandon outdated assumptions, embrace challenging growth experiences, and form new business relationships.

Leaders must be willing to embark on a deeply personal
process to engineer a new mindset. It takes small brave
moves to do this.

GROWTH AND FIXED MINDSETS

After decades of research, Stanford University psychologist Carol S. Dweck, PhD, author of *The Growth Mindset*, discovered a simple but groundbreaking idea: the power of mindset. She shows how success in school, work, sports, the arts, and almost every area of human endeavor can be dramatically influenced by how we think about our talents and abilities.

People with a *fixed mindset*—those who believe abilities are fixed—are less likely to flourish than those with a *growth mindset*—those who believe abilities can be developed. *Mindset* reveals how great leaders, parents, teachers, managers, and athletes can put this idea to use to foster outstanding accomplishments.

To briefly sum up the findings: Individuals who believe their talents can be developed (through hard work, good strategies, and input from others) have a growth mindset. They tend to achieve more than those with a more fixed mindset (those who believe their talents are innate gifts). This is because they worry less about looking smart and put more energy into learning. When entire companies embrace a growth mindset, their employees report feeling far more empowered and committed; they also receive far greater organizational support for collaboration and innovation. In contrast, people at primarily fixed-mindset companies report more of the following: lack of trust, cheating, and deception among employees, presumably to gain an advantage.[17]

Everyone is actually a mixture of fixed and growth mindsets, and that mixture continually evolves with experience. A "pure" growth mindset doesn't exist, which we must acknowledge to attain the benefits we seek. Leaders who embody a growth mindset encourage appropriate risk-taking, knowing some risks won't work out. They reward employees for important and useful lessons learned, even if a project does not meet its original goals. They support collaboration across organizational boundaries rather than competition among employees or units. They are committed to the growth of every member, not just in words but in deeds, such as broadly available development and advancement opportunities. They also continually reinforce growth mindset values with concrete policies.

We all have our own fixed-mindset triggers. When we face challenges, receive criticism, or fare poorly compared to others, we can easily fall into insecurity or defensiveness, which is a response that inhibits growth. Our work environments, too, can be full of fixed-mindset triggers. To remain in a growth zone, we must identify and work with these triggers. Many managers and executives have benefited from learning to recognize when their fixed-mindset "persona" shows up and what it says to make them feel threatened or defensive. Most importantly, over time they have a higher level of

---

17   Carol Dweck, *Mindset* (London: Robinson, an imprint of Constable & Robinson Ltd, 2017), 12.

awareness and can talk back to it, persuading it to collaborate with them as they pursue challenging goals.

LEARNING AND PERFORMANCE MINDSETS

A learning mindset involves being motivated toward increasing one's competence and mastering something new. A performance mindset involves being motivated toward gaining favorable judgments (or avoiding negative judgments) about one's competence. Leaders with a learning mindset, compared to those with a performance mindset, are more mentally primed to increase their competence, engage in deep-level learning strategies, seek out feedback, and exert more of an effort. They are also persistent, adaptable, willing to cooperate, and tend to perform at a higher level.[18]

Mindset is like momentum; it exists because of past behaviors and experiences and changes because of new behaviors and experiences.

BEHAVIOR

Leader behavior is the traits and characteristics that make someone an effective leader. Leaders utilize their behavior to help them guide, direct, and influence the work of their team. Many innate characteristics enhance leadership behavior. However, there are strategies and actions leaders can work to develop to improve their behavior and be more effective. Organizations thrive on leaders who use their behavior to

---

18 R. Gottfredson, "To Be a Great Leader You Need the Right Mindset," *Harvard Business Review*, January 17, 2020.

share a vision, encourage teams, and ensure everyone is as effective as possible.

Leadership is extremely important for an organization. Brave leaders help improve morale in an organization. Even during hard times, effective leaders can help their teams (and even peers) be confident and happy in their positions. Brave leaders also help retain employees. Turnover is expensive and disruptive in an organization, and good leadership is key in employees sticking around or jumping ship. As you likely already know, people don't quit jobs, they quit managers. Leaders help the company save money and increase productivity by keeping retention rates high.

Similarly, brave leaders can help nurture bravery in future leaders. They mentor and work with team members to help them grow in their role and be prepared for new roles within the company. This is good for everyone. Finally, brave leaders are instrumental in helping the company make money. More productive teams lead to more things being done, higher creativity, and better overall success for the organization.

In practice, it's easy to see the benefits of a good leader. Martin Luther King Jr., Gandhi, Oprah Winfrey, Bill Gates, and Arianna Huffington are all examples of people who impacted the world around them in positive ways. Looking at their leadership behaviors helps us understand the importance of the right traits and actions. These inspiring people's vision, perseverance, and commitment to their values helped them rise in the face of adversity and achieve almost impossible triumphs. What was their focus? Small brave moves have a compounding effect over time.

"Leadership is a series of behaviors rather than a role for heroes."

—MARGARET WHEATLEY

When it comes to changing behaviors in organizations, leaders often speak about changing the underlying beliefs and mindsets of people. Today, it has become so fashionable to talk about the role of mindsets in changing behaviors that people seem to have completely forgotten the simple formula. Behavior is a function of personality and environment, which was articulated by Kurt Lewin decades ago. Further, personality itself is shaped by environment. Hence, environment is too important in driving behavior to be ignored.[19]

HABITS

Highly successful leaders understand success in any form is not an event, it's a process. The most successful leaders understand success is something that is cultivated over time. Success is a daily grind and commitment that functions around your life purpose.

To stand out as a leader in your own right, you must create the habits that back your success and build your credibility. Once these habits become a part of your daily routine, you set yourself up to become the great leader of your own success and help others achieve their success.

---

19 Kurt Lewin, *Resolving Social Conflicts: Field Theory in Social Science* (Washington, DC: American Psychological Association, 1997), 10–15.

I interviewed Nate Legrand, president and CEO of Center-Point Financial Group, which he founded in 2000, for my Being Brave series, and we talked about the importance of our habits. "I think a lot of business owners tend to be workaholics, and Nicole, you know exactly what I'm talking about. So, in times like this, when you're working extra hard, and there's extra stress, I think it's more important than ever you protect your energy and protect your confidence. Number one for me is the simple things Mom and Dad taught us when we were young. Get sleep, make sure you're ready to go, and fight that battle you have coming the next day. So, I'm trying to get to bed by nine o'clock every night. My kids and my wife laugh at me a little bit, but it is important and essential to protect my energy so I'm ready to go. We've all heard fatigue makes cowards out of all of us. It is important to make sure our energy is there. We all need to be eating right, exercising, making sure we're ready to go and fight tomorrow's battle."

Overestimating the importance of one defining moment and underestimating the value of making small brave moves on a frequent basis is easy to do. We convince ourselves big success requires big action or big bravery. Whether it is building a business, writing a book, winning a championship, or achieving any other goal, we put pressure on ourselves to make some monumental improvement everyone will talk about. The small habits we do every day make the most impact.

In the book *Atomic Habits*, James Clear talks about how improving by 1 percent isn't particularly notable, some-times not even noticeable, but can be far more meaningful, especially in the long run. The difference a tiny improvement can make over time is astounding. Here is how the math works: if you can get 1 percent better each day for one year, you'll end up thirty-seven times better by the time you're done. Conversely, if you can get 1 percent worse each day for one year, you'll decline nearly down to zero. What starts as a small win or minor setback accumulates into something much more.[20]

Your habits can compound for you or against you.

> "Chains of habit are too light to be felt until they are too heavy to be broken."
>
> —WARREN BUFFET

Small brave moves are the compound interest of leadership. The same way money multiplies through compound interest, the effects of your mindsets, behaviors, and habits multiply as you repeat them. They may seem to make little difference in that moment or on any given day, yet the impact they deliver over months or years are the key to life-changing leadership.

Which mindsets, behaviors, and habits
are best serving you right now?

---

20 James Clear, *Atomic Habits an Easy & Proven Way to Build Good Habits and Bad Ones* (New York: Penguin Audio, an imprint of Penguin Random House Audio Publishing Group, 2019), 16.

Reflect here:

_____

_____

_____

_____

_____

Which mindsets, behaviors, and habits aren't serving you?

Reflect here:

_____

_____

_____

_____

_____

You are your greatest project

In the research I have done by interviewing leaders who lead with their bravest selves, I found they live by these principles:

- ☑ Start with Their Authentic Self
- ☑ Talk Straight
- ☑ Slips, Trips, Falls (Fail Fast)
- ☑ Lean on Others
- ☑ Be There for Others
- ☑ Be Intentional
- ☑ Relentless Curiosity
- ☑ Embrace Uncertainty
- ☑ Hope Drive
- ☑ Promote Team Sport
- ☑ Build a Culture of the Above

Little acts of bravery are the key to life-changing leadership. Each chapter takes a principle and explores mindsets, behaviors, and habits.

PART II

PRINCIPLES OF A BRAVER LEADER

3.

STARTS WITH SELF, YOUR AUTHENTIC SELF

———

"Tell All of Your Story. Every. Last. Bit."

—TIFFANY HADDISH

As I walked through the door of the Michigan Ross School of Business Executive Education Program, my heart was racing, and I was beaming from ear to ear. There I was, this young emerging leader, considered to be a high potential leader in my organization at the time. This was my first big investment in my professional development, and I was ready to soak it all in. The course was being taught by Dave Ulrich and Wayne Brockbank, two well-known human resources thought leaders, authors, and professors. I was ready to grow into a strategic human resources leader.

An added benefit of the trip was a short break from our very young family. We had three children within four years. Morgen was turning five, Joe turning three, and Nic turning two.

When we started a family, Dave and I had made the choice to work opposite shifts to allow the children to be home more versus being in daycare. Not to mention, evenings were where the action was for Dave. He was a sergeant leading the gang unit and special weapons and tactics unit (SWAT). He carried a pager and cell phone and was on call twenty-four/seven, which really meant he would go into work anytime between noon and 2:00 p.m. and come home anytime between 10:00 p.m. and midnight most days.

We were single parents for four days and together for his two days off. We both made sacrifices, which usually meant short nights for him and hectic evenings for me. The kids' and my evening routine would be coming home from daycare, making dinner, playing or exploring, baths, reading, rocking, and finally, bedtime. At this point I would look around the house, the mess, and determine if I had enough energy to put it back together before my bedtime.

Here's the deal: we wouldn't change it for the world. A consequence of the busyness is there was never any down time or reflection time. This trip, unbeknownst to me at the time, afforded me just that. This trip would open something I had been bottling up for years in my subconscious mind.

Content Warning: sexual abuse.

The days were packed with deep learning and the evenings were quiet, reflective, and restful. During the second evening, I awoke in the middle of the night with a nightmarish dream, one I have had off and on for as long as I can remember. I could not make out many details, but there were enough to begin to pause and think. *What happened to me? What does it mean?* I grabbed a pen and paper and captured every detail I could remember.

The next day, I was distracted off and on throughout the day as I was beginning to remember more and more. I remembered a young male. I remembered I was yelling and screaming. I remembered his pants down. I remembered him locking me alone in a room. I realized there may be one person who would know more about this—my mom. I found my way back to my hotel room after yet another long day of learning how to think strategically. I told myself, one small brave move. I couldn't bring myself to call my mom, but instead texted her. It was really the bravest move in the moment, just to begin a conversation about this.

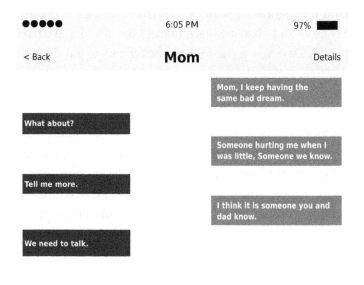

●●●●●   6:05 PM   97% ▬▬

< Back   **Mom**   Details

Mom, I keep having the same bad dream.

What about?

Someone hurting me when I was little, Someone we know.

Tell me more.

I think it is someone you and dad know.

We need to talk.

At this moment, I was feeling light-headed, nauseous, and I was in shock. These dreams, these nightmares, all these years—this is real.

I landed back home on Friday after a long week and was met with the biggest hugs and kisses from the kids and Dave. My mom and I had arranged to meet the next day at a park to talk. Dave was going to drop me off and go put the kids down for a nap after a full morning. This park was a shared favorite place of ours.

My mom and I have always had a strong relationship, except for those few years in my early twenties when I knew everything, and she knew nothing. She was always there for me, teaching me, loving me, and caring for me. She never missed an opportunity to attend my sporting events, programs, or competitions. As an adult, she showed up in important ways, helping us with the kids when I would travel or when we needed to sneak out for an evening. She was always a strong presence in our lives. More than just a mom, she was a close friend, someone I could go to for almost anything.

Next small brave move was a face-to-face conversation. I wasn't sure I was ready for my mom to fill in the blanks of this story.

She first wanted to know what I remembered. I felt like I was going to throw up right there. Slowly, with my voice shaking, I said, "I remember the first incident started off in our bathroom, his pants were down, and he was forceful and yelling. I remember crying. The next time he locked me in our porch playroom. I knew he was going to try to hurt me again. I remember screaming and trying to defend myself. To punish me, he would throw me on top of this tall antique dresser. He would lock me inside that room, leaving me all alone and scared, all for fighting back. He would only come back to 'check on me,' ultimately making further demands of me and only releasing me when my parents were close to returning." As I shared these nightmares with my mom, we were both crying. She realized I remembered everything.

He was fifteen; I was five. He was my uncle; I was his niece. He lived in Davenport, Iowa, but stayed with our family that summer. My uncle would watch us when my parents would go out over the course of the summer, and this is when the abuse would happen.

My mom was surprised at the responses from doctors and her family when she took a stand. Shortly after "the uncle" had left, my five-year-old self had come to her momma telling her what had happened. She immediately acted, reaching out to our family doctor. She had been told by our family doctor to never speak of it again and as a result, I would forget it.

I was young and would never remember what the doctor said. It was 1977.

She immediately called her father to gain support to address the issue at hand. He refused; my mom called him a coward. Because of his response, my mom severed ties with him and that side of the family for about fifteen years. I never knew the reason he wasn't in our lives. It was our version of normal. We never really spoke to many of the people on my mom's side of the family, except for one of her other brothers and a sister in Florida. Now, I understand why.

Her father wasn't much of a father and her mother wasn't much of a mother; parenting wasn't on either of their agendas. Years of alcohol and drug abuse fueled with depression caused much dysfunction in her family. My guess is the abuse from my uncle didn't start and stop with me, either.

She protected me from it ever happening again. She was the oldest of over then siblings, and all but one were stepsiblings or half siblings. She left her home at age sixteen, dropping out of school in ninth grade to make a better life for herself, and she did. She worked hard, obtained her GED, married my dad at only seventeen, and they built a beautiful life and business together. She broke the cycle. How? Small brave moves.

Why this moment for this to reveal itself? Why now, this awakening? Then I realized it happened when I was five years old, the same age as my beautiful daughter, Moe. Looking at her, I couldn't even imagine what my five-year-old self went through. It made me hold her even tighter, protect her even more. I could not and would not let this happen to her, Joe, or Nic.

I am not sharing this story for sympathy or pity. I share it because at a young age, I learned the importance of small brave moves and the importance of practicing bravery: standing up in the moment and telling my mom, then bringing it up to my mom years later, telling my husband, sitting around the fire pit at the lake telling my lifelong friends, telling my brothers who were so young and likely in just the other room while it was happening, the importance of seeing a therapist and working through it. It takes bravery to confront the things inside you, to discover trauma in your psyche you'd been holding onto for a long time, to be brave enough to talk about it, and to start working through it.

"Self-awareness is a superpower. Know yourself and be yourself."

—JIM KWIK, *LIMITLESS*

PERSONAL HISTORIES
When I am working with a newly formed leadership team or even a team who may not have invested the time up front in getting to know each other, I have several exercises I love that are powerful and create strong momentum for the team.

One in particular was inspired by Patrick Lencioni's Five Dysfunctional Teams.[21] I took it and modified it, experimenting with how to make it better, stronger, and even more impactful. Each leader does a six-minute monologue talking about their happiest moments, saddest moments, and why they are here. The basic rules are the leader must fill the six minutes or the team sits in silence until the six minutes are complete. It is a monologue. You can't ask questions. You aren't allowed to talk about your resume or CV; nobody cares. Get personal, go deep, and get past the rehearsed crap we always tell everyone.

In return, every single time, I get looks of panic and horror followed by nervous laughter and jokes being made about trust falls. Then we move into the exercise and what happens is profound.

Recently, I was working with a CEO and her leadership team. She had just filled her open C-suite roles, increasing her leadership team by 50 percent. She is a visionary with big plans to grow the business she leads. She recognized quickly her leadership was becoming divided between the new regime and the old regime. Note, the old regime had one year of experience in the business ahead of the new regime. Regardless, it was creating some tension within the team.

The CEO and I carefully crafted an offsite for the team. They were so busy working on "what" they needed to deliver, they were missing the "how" they wanted to deliver the

21   Patrick Lencioni, *The Five Dysfunctions of a Team* (San Francisco: Jossey Bass, 2002).

strategy—how to work best together. About midmorning, I introduced the personal histories exercise. I asked the CEO to go first. She role modeled vulnerability like a pro, which opened the door for the rest of her team to do the same. Each executive jumped into the six minutes sharing their personal stories, the most powerful stories.

Most times there isn't a dry eye by then end, not just from those telling their story but also those listening to others' stories we have never learned from each other because we interact briefly and professionally. Once we learn each other's stories, we can better appreciate and understand how we approach certain things. We have to tell our stories, our personal stories, because it's the only way for people to get to know who we really are!

We have to start with our self, our authentic self.

When we aren't able to be brave enough, we don't show up as our true selves.

We have to be aligned to our truest self.

To understand how to lead others, you must understand people, and to understand people, you must understand yourself. Self-discovery often happens when we move out of our comfort zone and change the norm. Here is to the beginning of the journey.

BEST SELF ENABLES YOU TO BE YOUR AUTHENTIC SELF

When we ask leaders to take an assessment as a part of our leadership programs, a common question I get is, "Nicole, should I take this as the person I am at work or at home?" I always ask back, "Are you really two different people?" This question almost always forces a pause.

Your Authentic Self Defined: who you truly are as a person, regardless of your occupation, regardless of the influence of others. It is an honest representation of you. To be authentic means not caring what others think about you. To be authentic is to be true to yourself through your thoughts, words, and actions.

We are constantly balancing inner and outer aspects of ourselves to better fit in, to become more successful, or to find friendships. We are driven to find "our place" in society, and we want to be respected for who we truly are and what we have to contribute. Many of us are propelled even further, desiring to know and live our purpose, to find deeper meaning in our lives, and to feel the fulfillment that comes from becoming a more authentic person.

But at the same time, we live in a society that values superficiality, that strives for perfection, and defines success by the home we own, the vehicles we drive, or the dollars in our bank account and not by how well we live our values every day. So how are we supposed to be authentic in spite of the messages trying to convince us to be someone else?

How do I share more of who I am?

As leaders, it is important for us to not just show up as authentic but also create an environment for our teams to be authentic too! I was facilitating a leadership program and we were in the middle of a simulation. A manager was dealing with an issue with a team member by strictly sticking to the facts and business. The issue was the team member was running late most days and ducking out from time to time. The leader was in corporate robotic mode while trying to address the lateness and having to abruptly leave work. I paused the manager in the middle of the conversation and asked, "What are you most curious about right now?" in relation to the situation he was dealing with. He said, "I really want to understand more of what is happening for them and how I might be able to help." *Bingo!* Make the ask! Sometimes we play too high, and sometimes we play too low.

If you're going to manage and collaborate, you need to be both authoritative and approachable.

Keith Johnstone, a pioneer in improv theatre, lays out the difference between "playing high" and "playing low."

People who play high (think Judi Dench as Queen Elizabeth):

- Speak in complete sentences
- Keep their head still (imagine a police officer at a traffic stop)
- Hold eye contact when speaking as a method of intimidation

- Occupy as much space as possible (draping arms over chairs)
- Do not check others' eyes for reactions, and do not react to others
- Do not hesitate to interrupt
- Do not explain themselves, even when they speak cryptically

People who play low (think Woody Allen in almost any movie):

- Speak with higher voices (your voice is lower when you're relaxed)
- Speak in incomplete sentences
- Speak breathlessly or haltingly
- Lean forward
- Make fleeting, jerky motions, including glancing and looking away
- Smile more (a gesture of appeasement)
- Try to take up as little space as possible
- Check for approval
- Shout in attempts to intimidate (indicates an expectation of resistance)
- Explain themselves

Playing high correlates to being authoritative.[22]

To be more authentic, to be approachable, pull back on playing high and incorporate some—not many—of the playing

---

22 Keith Johnstone, *Impro: Improvisation and the Theatre*, (New York City: Routledge, 2015), 43–45.

low characteristics; lean forward, smile more (not in appeasement), and check for approval.

Brave Leaders regularly build on their past successes and achievements. In other words, they learn from what they have already accomplished to make the most of the current situation they find themselves in.

WHY LEADERS STRUGGLE WITH AUTHENTICITY

The word "authentic" traditionally referred to any work of art that is an original, not a copy. When used to describe leadership, of course, it has other meanings—and they can be problematic. For example, the notion of adhering to one's "true self" flies in the face of much research on how people evolve with experience, discovering facets of themselves they would never have unearthed through introspection alone. Being utterly transparent—disclosing every single thought and feeling—is both unrealistic and risky.

Stanford psychologist Deborah Gruenfeld describes this as managing the tension between authority and approachability. To be authoritative, you privilege your knowledge, experience, and expertise over the team's, maintaining a measure of distance. To be approachable, you emphasize your relationships with people, their input, their perspective, and you lead with empathy and warmth. Getting the balance right presents an acute authenticity crisis for true-to-selfers who typically have a strong preference for behaving one way or the other.[23]

---

23 Herminia Ibarra, "The Authenticity Paradox: Why Feeling like a Fake Can Be a Sign of Growth," *Harvard Business Review,* January 2015.

According to Herminia Ibarra, professor of organization behavior at the London School of Business, going against our natural inclinations can make us feel like impostors. We tend to latch on to authenticity as an excuse for sticking with what's comfortable. But few jobs allow us to do that for long. That's doubly true when we advance in our careers or when demands or expectations change.[24]

Leadership transitions require all of us to move way beyond our comfort zones. At the same time, however, they trigger a strong impulse to protect our identities. When we are unsure of ourselves or our ability to perform well or measure up in a new setting, we often retreat to familiar behaviors and styles. Ibarra's research also demonstrates the moments that most challenge our sense of self are the ones that can teach us the most about leading effectively.[25] By viewing ourselves as works in progress and evolving our professional identities through trial and error, we can develop a personal style that feels right to us and suits our organizations' changing needs.

I had designed and facilitated a retreat for a new executive leader at Darden Restaurants. He was transitioning to this new role and needed to build trust and set expectations for transformation to occur. I had designed a new exercise, "Authentic Self," to launch the retreat, which I had never done quite this way before. In the exercise, you answer six personal questions about yourself.

---

24 Ibid.
25 Ibid.

For the exercise to work, you need someone to kick it off and demonstrate vulnerability.

The executive leader agreed he should go first.

We were in this breathtaking space right on Vero Beach in Florida, the ideal spot for a retreat. We launched the day and moved into the exercise. He launched into his story by answering the six questions. One of the questions tugged at his heart, and you could hear his voice begin to quiver. He shared with us that during his childhood, he watched his sister battle leukemia and lose her life at the age of twelve. There was not a dry eye in our room that morning.

He went on to share he wasn't looking for sympathy about losing his sister. He felt honored to have had her in his life as long as he did. He wanted his new team to know about the experience so they would be informed of how he leads and how important family and caring for each other is. He wanted them to know they are a part of his family and he would be there for him. He was demonstrating how important their well-being was to him and the fragility of the lives he was responsible for.

It takes small brave moves because learning, by definition, starts with unnatural and often superficial behaviors that can make us feel calculating instead of genuine and spontaneous. But the only way to avoid being pigeonholed and ultimately become better leaders is to do the things that a rigidly authentic sense of self would keep us from doing.

HOW TO DEVELOP AUTHENTICITY

First, recognize your adaptive versus authentic self. The adaptive self is for helping you function through difficult and confusing times. The authentic self keeps you whole, real, and self-confident.[26] Observe how your "adaptive self" behaves, what it believes, how it reacts under pressure, and how it responds to challenges. Practice noticing which of these responses feel authentic, and which ones feel inauthentic. Take a moment and capture the feeling within notes on your phone, a small notepad, or voice recorder. By identifying which responses are adaptive versus authentic, you can begin to notice the falseness and begin to see the glimmers of truth underneath.

Authenticity and purpose are closely linked. A deep sense of purpose can help you to express your authenticity, while developing authenticity will often help you discover your purpose! You may discover the courage of your convictions and want to burst forward with passion to accomplish some worthy goal that moves you deeply enough to champion some sort of positive change. Open yourself up to living authentically, and your purpose is likely to become clearer.

In my executive coaching work, many leaders have not done the deep work. They take the easy way out and begin to adapt to the organization's mission, vision, and values. They are not yours, but there's nothing wrong with aligning with them. If you don't take the time to invest in building your purpose

---

26 Tchiki Davis, "Develop Authenticity: 20 Ways to Be a More Authentic Person," *Psychology Today,* April 15, 2019.

and values, you will wake up one day asking, *how did I get here? What am I doing?*

Have you aligned your life with your purpose? Have you done the deep work to figure out what it is?

YOUR PURPOSE—WHY ARE YOU HERE?

Having a purpose in life may decrease your risk of dying early, according to a study published in May 2019.

Researchers analyzed data from nearly seven thousand American adults between the ages of fifty-one and sixty-one who filled out psychological questionnaires on the relationship between mortality and life purpose. What they found shocked them, according to Celeste Leigh Pearce, one of the authors of the study published in *JAMA Current Open*. People who didn't have a strong life purpose—which was defined as "a self-organizing life aim that stimulates goals"—were more likely to die than those who did, and they were specifically more likely to die of cardiovascular diseases.[27]

Answering this question is a process and not a goal. It may take years of effort to truly hone in on your purpose, so you might as well start now. Get started by quickly writing down the answer to the following five questions:

---

27 Mara Gordon, "What's Your Purpose? Finding a Sense of Meaning in Life Is Linked to Health," *NPR*, May 25, 2019.

Answering this question is a process and not a goal. It may take years of effort to truly hone in on your purpose....so you might as well start now

Your Purpose

· · · · · · · · · · ●●●●●●●●●●●●●●● · · · · · · · ·

Why are you here?

What energizes you?

What drives you?

Who do you want to help?

What do you want to help with?

PERSONAL ETHOS, YOUR VALUES

Your ethos/values form the foundation of your life. They dictate the choices you make and determine the direction your life takes. Your values will influence your decisions related to your relationships, work, and other activities you engage in. Yet despite this importance, few people, including leaders, choose their values. Instead, they simply adopt the values of their parents and/or the dominant values of society. In all likelihood, the values you internalized as a child remain with you through adulthood (yes, in some cases people reject the values of their upbringings). Unfortunately, these values may also have created a life that is carrying you down a path that is not the direction you want to go.

I remember one of my mom's ethos was tradition. Why? She grew up in a family where traditions didn't exist. When she and my dad married and started a family of their own, creating traditions was very important to them. After losing both of them, I held on as tightly as I could to the traditions she had created. I was met with resistance from both of my brothers. Sometimes, the resistance was one of them cancelling at the last minute or another one showing up just to check the tradition box. It was hard for all of us. I realized after a couple of years and a few rounds of traditions, it was time to bless and release the old traditions that no longer served our family and give myself permission to start new ones.

Personal ethos is a reminder of how you want to live your life so you can deliver on your purpose. It is a personal floatation device you reach for when things aren't going as planned. It should also keep your ego in check when the wind is at your back.

"All of us actually do have a personal ethos—we just may not be able to clearly articulate it. But we do have a pattern of values, motivations, and aspirations that be distilled from decisions, both large and small, that we have made in our lives. We are what we decide, how we behave, and what we do—much more so than what we say, what we intend, or what we think we want. This pattern makes up the 'personal ethos' by which we live, consciously or unconsciously."

—BOB SCHOULTZ, RETIRED NAVY SEAL OFFICER

Imagine you are doing what brings you the most joy, spending time with the people you love, using your natural strengths and talents, and using your gifts to their fullest. You are feeling incredibly fulfilled and you are living according to what you truly value the most. Discovering your ethos allows you to take a stand for what is important to you, and to make decisions and choices based on what is important. Living your values is inherently fulfilling, even when it is hard.

For example, if authenticity is one of your values, you may find there are times when it feels uncomfortable to fully live according to that value. However, it is important to remember the discomfort will eventually pass and a sense of integrity or congruency with this value will remain. When a value is not being honored, however, we can often feel an internal tension or dissonance.

Have you ever been in a situation when you were doing something in conflict with your ethos? Was there a time when you may have floated to the tone of a discussion versus taking a position or voicing your concern? Have you ever been inconsistent in conversations you are having with others to gain alignment with them? It takes small brave moves to say, "Wait a minute..."

Getting clear on your ethos is important. Take the time to explore which ones are most important.

Big areas to consider when writing a personal ethos:

☑ What brings you joy? What makes things fun?
☑ How does community play a role in your ethos?
☑ Are there any challenges you have been facing you need to address?
☑ How do you fill your cup? How do you rejuvenate?
☑ Have there been any hardships or tragedies you want to recognize and be more intentional about?
☑ How does nature play a role for you?
☑ What about failure or not getting what you want?
☑ What role does faith play for you?

168 CORE VALUES   Bravium

Acceptance	Decisiveness	Hospitality
Accomplishment	Delivery Results	Humility
Accountability	Dependability	Imagination
Accuracy	Development	Improvementu
Adaptability	Diligence	Independence
Agility	Defectiveness	Individuality
Alertness	Discipline	Influence
Ambition	Discretion	Innovation
Authenticity	Diversity	Inspiration
Availability	Drive	Integrity
Awareness	Ecology	Intelligence
Brilliance	Education	International
Capability	Efficiency	Invention
Carefulness	Endurance	Investment
Curiosity	Enthusiasm	Involvement
Clearness	Equality	Justice
Cleverness	Esteem	Kindness
Commitment	Ethical Practice	Knowledge
Communication	Excellence	Leadership
Competence	Expectation	Loyalty
Confidence	Experience	Motivation
Continuity	Fairness	Objectivity
Consistency	Faithfulness	Openness
Cooperation	Flexibility	Optimism
Courage	Freedom	Order
Creativity	Generosity	Organization
Curiosity	Gratitude	Originality
Customer Focus	Honesty	Participation

168 CORE VALUES   Bravium

Passion	Reputation	Supervision
Patience	Resilience	Support
Perception	Resolution	Sustainability
Performance	Respect	Synergy
Persistence	Responsibility	Talent
Persuasion	Responsiveness	Teamwork
Philanthropy	Results-oriented	Thoroughness
Potency	Rigor	Timeliness
Power	Risk Taking	Tolerance
Practice	Satisfaction	Toughness
Precision	Security	Tradition
Preparation	Sensitivity	Training
Preservation	Serenity	Transparency
Pride	Seriousness	Trustworthiness
Productivity	Significance	Truth
Professionalism	Simplicity	Uniqueness
Profitability	Sincerity	Unity
Progress	Skillfulness	Utility
Prosperity	Solidity	Valor
Public Service	Sophistication	Value
Punctuality	Spirit	Variety
Purity	Spontaneity	Virtue
Quality	Stability	Vision
Rationality	Standard	Vitality
Realty	Straightness	Warmth
Recognition	Strenght	Wealth
Reflection	Structure	Wisdom
Reliability	Success	Zest

Write down a few words or phrases that come to mind as you articulate your personal ethos.

_____

_____

_____

Start with three to five, but no more. Then focus on living those to the fullest.

My ethos help guide me to live my purpose. I look at them every day. I figure out ways to bring them even more into my daily life. Knowing your ethos is crucial to being authentic.

Have you done the deep work? If not, it is never too late. Start now with one small brave move.

Brave Leaders do the deep discovery work in understanding our authentic selves, how we want to show up, and how we want to be. The clarity will give you a path forward to living your best life.

4.

TALKING STRAIGHT— HOW SPICY DO YOU WANT IT?

Shoot it to me straight, no chaser.

Imagine you are being interviewed for a new leadership role. In that interview you're told, "If you can't fix the area you will be responsible for, we will outsource the whole thing." *Whoa!* Outsource it all? Seriously? It was risky, but you know what else is risky? Getting braces later in life. I was up for the challenge.

Just thirty days later, I was meeting with the CEO over a fancy lunch to present my ninety-day plan. We were both having salads. We finished our meal, and for about an hour we discussed my ninety-day plan.

As we were finishing up, the CEO told me, "Great job," and it was exactly what I needed to hear. Telling me I did a great job meant we were on track, right? I was walking back to my office, stopping by my team's cubicles to check in and say hello. Just when I sat down at my desk, I heard a loud and obnoxious *ping!* A member of my team, whom I just said hello to, messaged me this: "Nicole, you may want to check your braces. I think you have something in them."

My heart fell as I was thinking, *wait, what?* There was no mirror in my office, so I dashed to the bathroom to check out the situation. As I looked into the mirror and paused, horror ran through me. Staring back at me was a large leaf of lettuce that had wrapped itself around my front bracket, protecting them almost like a mouth guard. I was gagging as I saw the bright green color of the lettuce had transitioned to dark green and gross!

I hit replay on the events since lunch in my mind.

1. We were both eating salads at lunch.
2. We reviewed my ninety-day plan—*wait,* the lettuce had to have been there the entire hour I was reviewing my plan. Yet didn't say anything—*nothing,* nada, zilch.
3. I walked back to my office showcasing lettuce in my braces to everyone I spoke to.

Wait, why didn't he say anything? He wasn't necessarily polite, either. Remember, he was the one who told me he would outsource the department if we couldn't turn it around. Yet, he simply couldn't tell me about lettuce in my braces. How could I know he would give me feedback on our risky situation if he wasn't able to share something so basic as, "You have lettuce in your teeth."

Why do we struggle having these conversations? Why can't we let someone know they have something on their shirt, or their zipper is down, or there is something in their teeth? Why do we make it so awkward? It makes the even tougher conversations we need to have almost insurmountable.

Do you say something or let it go?

I allowed my inner critic to come out to "judge" the situation. Here is what the critic had to say: *Nicole, you left a role where you had strong credibility and a track record of producing results for this? To work for a company who wants to outsource a department where the CEO won't give you feedback? Can you even trust him? Maybe you have you been set up to fail.*

Then I set the inner critic aside and thought, *maybe I have to be brave for the CEO to consider being brave.*

This CEO isn't alone. I have coached over a thousand leaders, executives, and CEOs, and this is a common theme. I was recently coaching a CEO who shared a story that really changed the trajectory of her career, which was a moment where a colleague shot it to her straight. Her role was leading clinical and cultural transformation over a large region, moving from physician-centered care to patient-centered care. Her previous experience working in the army, overseas, and stateside taught her to work with the resources available—period. You have to move forward, no matter what. After much success in this role, she was getting ready to transition to her new role when a peer from her team said to her:

"You are destined for something more. Even this next position isn't it. You lead your teams telling them to work at the top of their license, to be all in, yet you *engineer yourself to be small.*"

She had a big job and was moving into an even bigger role. Her peer wasn't wrong, though. She ruminated for quite a while on his message. She realized she had been working below her capabilities, was overqualified in her roles, and was just killing it in every role. That moment of straight talk triggered something much bigger in her, and she went after her first CEO role—the current role she holds—which is in the process of transforming health care at a national level. Why did he share this with her? Because he cared and saw something she wasn't seeing.

CARE PERSONALLY, CHALLENGE DIRECTLY

Radical Candor is on my top ten list of favorite books. The model resonates with so many leaders. To illustrate radical candor in action, author Kimberly Scott shares a story about a time her boss criticized her. "I had just joined Google and gave a presentation to the founders and the CEO about how the AdSense business was doing. I walked in feeling a little nervous, but happily the business was on fire. When we told Larry, Sergey, and Eric how many publishers we had added over the previous months, and Eric almost fell off his chair and asked what resources they could give us to help continue this amazing success. So… I sort of felt like the meeting went okay."

But after the meeting, Scott's boss, Sheryl Sandberg, suggested they take a walk together. She talked about the things she liked about the presentation and how impressed she was with the success the team was having—yet Scott could feel a "but" coming. "Finally, she said, 'But you said *um* a lot.' I thought, 'Oh, no big deal. I know I do that. But who cares if I said *um* when I had the tiger by the tail?'"

Sandberg pushed forward, asking whether Scott's *ums* were the result of nervousness. She even suggested Google could hire a speaking coach to help. Still, Scott brushed off the concern; it didn't seem like an important issue. "Finally, Sheryl said, 'You know, Kim, I can tell I'm not really getting through to you. I'm going to have to be clearer here. When you say *um* every third word, it makes you sound stupid.' Now, *that* got my attention!" Scott said.[28]

Care personally and challenge directly is exactly what Sandberg did. Scott knows now it was the kindest thing Sandberg could have done for her. "If she hadn't said it just that way, I would've kept blowing her off. I wouldn't have addressed the problem, and what a silly thing to let trip you up." Scott did work with that speaking coach and kicked her *um* habit handily. In the years since, Scott has worked to operationalize what it was that made Sandberg such a great boss.[29]

---

28 Kimberly Scott, *Radical Candor: Be a Kick-Ass Boss Without Losing Your Humanity* (New York: St Martin's Press, 2017), 10–12.

29 Ibid.

It sounds so simple to say bosses need to tell employees when they're screwing up. But it very rarely happens.

Yes, and it gets even harder the higher we climb in our organizations. It becomes much riskier if it is not a lived operating norm. I remember wrapping up a meeting with our executive team and the CAO, Jim, pulled me aside afterward to ask me how I thought it went. I had just finished presenting and recommending a big change to our benefits plans. I had done deep strategic work pulling in the best experts and advisors to help me evaluate and create the best solution. I was confident in the change yet knew it would likely be met with some resistance. I responded I thought it went well but was concerned with the lack of dialogue around the recommendation. It was difficult to read the room.

He started with, "Your recommendation is well thought out and absolutely the move we need to make, but I want you to be aware though as you went in for the ask and to close us on it, your voice changed and trailed off to a high-pitched voice. It leaves me and likely others uncertain and not confident in the recommendation you just made because you don't seem confident yourself."

Right when he said it, I knew he was right. I was playing too low. I remember feeling it the moment he spoke of it, too. Why, why did I do that? I was confident in my recommendation but not confident in the people in the room. I learned a lot from Jim taking time to talk straight with me that day. I began to invest more time in designing "the close" of my presentations as I had the beginnings. I learned by scanning the room with my eyes and sensing doubt or concern to lean into it and open the dialogue versus letting it play out in how I was presenting.

One of our operating principles at Bravium HD is **Talk Straight.** When my business partner Jeff and I created our operating principles, we knew what type of relationship and culture we wanted to build from the start. We knew it was important to create an intentional and valued environment from the beginning. We have both worked in roles inside departments or on teams where being honest or talking straight just wasn't valued or encouraged. Now, working externally with clients, we see where they aren't quite sure how to do it. They believe in it conceptually and need help doing it. We believe if we can model what it looks like successfully, we can help build stronger cultures where it lives and thrives.

Here is our definition of what it means:

> Talk straight: Be honest. Tell the truth. Let people know where you stand. Use simple language. Call things what they are. Demonstrate integrity. Don't manipulate people or distort facts. Don't spin the truth. Don't leave false impressions. Do it because you care about the person and the situation. Always say it with heart.

Right from the start, we would have talk straight conversations as we designed what we wanted our relationship and our business model to look like, focusing on not just the "what" we wanted to accomplish together, but also the "how." I appreciated how it always comes from the heart, too. Nothing festers. We listen, we adjust, and we move on—yesterday, today, and tomorrow.

I remember one of our first talk straight conversations occurred at our favorite Starbucks spot. We would meet for hours every week designing and planning our business. There was something different about this morning, though. Jeff started off the conversation asking permission to talk straight and went on to share how another member of our team was making him feel, and it had been going on for a few months. He had tried to work through it and, unfortunately, he knew he could no longer work with her.

It was uncomfortable for Jeff because she had joined the team first and she also happened to be a longtime friend of mine. He knew by having this conversation with me, he and I might not work together any longer. He brought to light an issue that had been festering. It wasn't anyone's fault, yet it needed to be addressed. Because we had the conversation early, we were able to discuss the best course of action for our business and team.

I have grown tremendously from these conversations because many times Jeff might see something I had not, and many times I see things Jeff may not be seeing. We serve each other well in our partnership in this way. You must not only be brave enough to give it, but brave enough to receive it.

We wanted to have the same relationship with our clients. We began to weave it into the beginning of our work with clients. I soon realized when we started to talk straight with a client, we were able to foster much deeper relationships.

We were about a year into living our operating principles when a CEO asked us to come in and help his team work better together. I asked questions to better understand the dynamic and the role of the CEO in this.

He said,

> **"Oh Nicole, you can't fix me. I am who I am. I just need you to fix them so we can deliver the results we need."**

The challenger side of me sees something that is failing and can immediately envision what success could look like and create a path to get there. Now, overlay it with my twelve years of experience at Conagra Foods where I was strategically placed in a new role, in a department, plant, or business that was struggling every twenty-four months with the orders to get in there and fix it. The upside of moving roles quickly was that around the time we were starting to slide into a thrive and maintenance mode, I was moved to the next adventure. The downside of moving roles too quickly was I never had the opportunity to make the small shifts you need to make to refine the initial solution you put into place.

Listening to this CEO, my mind was sorting through solutions: *I can get them working better together, I can fix this, so put me in coach!* It was instinctive. I had done it before and could do it again. What I soon learned in the days following was I couldn't fix this without starting with him. He and I needed to be aligned on him modeling what he was looking for, but we weren't. This was the moment to have a talk straight conversation with the CEO to let him know he had to be a part of the solution for this to work. We would need him to model what he expected of the leadership team, but he refused. He wanted to outsource all the responsibility to me. I let him know I would be refunding his large retainer and wished him the very best. Sometimes, an outcome of talking straight ends in blessing and releasing.

Brave Leaders summon the courage to deliver important messages with bravery and grace!

HOW TO TALK STRAIGHT

Leaders, Brave Leaders, conceptually get Talk Straight yet struggle with the "how to" part.

I teach straight talk at nearly every strategy, culture, or leadership session I lead. I do so because it's often the barrier between good and great teams. Talk straight is about being honest, telling the truth, and letting people know where you stand.

Makes sense, right?

Believing it in principle is easy. Practicing it is another thing. Most leaders believe in it but fail to practice. The thing about straight talk is it requires a tremendous amount of bravery and grace to do it. It's like ordering dinner at a Thai restaurant. You know how the wait staff asks, "How spicy do you want it?"

How spicy do you want it?

Level 10 is the spiciest you can get! It includes a warning label that reads "caution you might EXPLODE."
It might feel like your career is on the line. Survival mentality.
"Better to live to fight another day!"

What would it take to talk straight at 5 or 6?

Level 1 is safe and easy, like being in a meeting with watching someone struggle and not say something, and maybe even thinking thank goodness its not me.

But let me ask you a question.

Which level of straight talk do you think gives you the best chance to make a difference in your organization? Why don't we fight for our right to talk straight?

Three reasons:

1. We are not sure what or how to say it.
2. We care too much about what others think or say.
3. We believe we will get politically fired, where you are dead to them but still work there.

It's a big decision, or is it?

Let's look at some conversation starters to address the "not sure what or how to say it."

- Can I share something with you that may be uncomfortable for you and for me?
- I want to make you quickly aware of something you may not be aware of...
- I care about you; I want to let you know something I am seeing...
- Can I share something with you that you may not be seeing?
- I am invested in you and I'd like to give you my reaction to...

Your language should be simple, clear, direct, and neutral. Don't say things like, "I feel so bad about saying this," or, "This is really hard for me to do," because it takes the focus away from the problem and toward your own neediness. While this can be hard, this language can make your counterpart feel obligated to focus on making you feel better before moving on.

One of my closest friends, Kristi, calls it hard truths. She shares with me when she has had to deliver some hard truths to her husband, a coworker, or even a close friend. We had been hearing rumors the husband of a friend of ours was cheating on our friend. Then the rumors turned into facts. Kristi was the one who delivered the hard truth to let her know what we knew. She won't keep the hard truths from you even if you don't want to hear the bad news. She delivers small hard truths that occur daily or weekly, too. Kristi wants to be able to be open and honest with you and expects the same in return. I love her for it.

Trust the silence. Don't erase the awkwardness.

If you are going to ask a powerful question, then do it.

Follow it with silence.

You need to manage yourself. Silence gets you out of the way and creates a space others will fill in themselves. Silence is often uncomfortable or awkward. We are not very familiar with it, and in everyday conversation, we usually try to fill the gaps. Silence is a form of communication. It has many faces, can mean different things to different people, can communicate different things, and its meaning depends on the context. Even though there are times the use of silence can block communication, there is also the constructive use of silence, which enhances and strengthens it.

Pause and play beats inside your head to a rhythm. Usually by the eighth to tenth beat, they will fill the silence, trust me.

This kind of silence provides a safe place where the person can grow and open up. The focus is on them. This silence conveys empathy, respect, reflective listening, and support.

Tips:

1. Don't be afraid or intimidated by long periods of silence.
2. Silence is a dynamic process. Don't try to fill the gaps.
3. Periods of silence may symbolize the importance of an issue.

YES, AND!

Improv has mastered the art of "Yes, and" build on what each person is saying! *Say "and," not "but."* When you need to disagree with someone, express your contrary opinion as "and." It's not necessary for someone else to be wrong for you to be right. When you're surprised to hear something your counterpart has said, don't interject with a "But that's not right!" Just add your perspective.

TALK STRAIGHT FRAMEWORKS:

START/STOP/CONTINUE:

This is a great tool and method of feedback to use one-on-one or in teams.

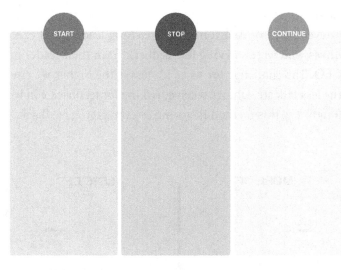

Instructions: List two things you would like to see the person start, two things you would like them to continue, and one thing you would like them to stop.

Who can use this?

- One-on-one Leader to Direct Report and a Direct Report to a Leader
- Team—everyone completes one for everyone and you verbally share in three-to four-minute rounds, one-on-one with each other. At the end, you review all of the feedback and look for themes, taking away the top three things you should continue and the top three things you should consider doing differently.
- Cross Functionally—this could work well in project teams following the steps above as a team as well.

MORE OF/LESS OF:

I developed this early on while coaching leaders and executives who were starving for feedback from their leader or CEO. The challenge for us as leaders is the higher we rise, the less talk straight we receive. Asking for feedback can be tough. Try this method in asking or even giving feedback.

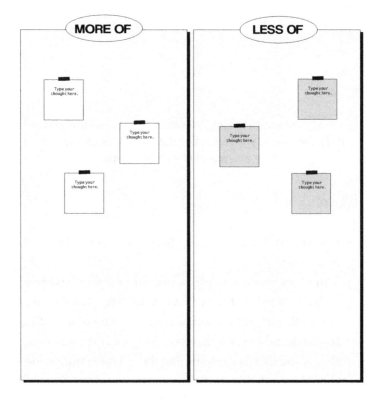

Instructions: Ask, what specifically should I be doing more of? What specifically should I be doing less of? Consider asking for three comments on each.

Who can use this?

- One-on-one Leader to Direct Report and a Direct Report to a Leader
- Team—everyone completes one for everyone and you verbally share in three-to four-minute rounds, one-on-one with each other. At the end, you review all of the feedback and look for themes, taking away the top three things you should continue and the top three things you should consider doing differently.
- Cross Functionally—this could work well in project teams following the steps above as a team as well.

CONTINUE AND CONSIDER

General Electric (GE) introduced a new feedback framework in 2015 to focus on behavioral change instead of the traditional "strength" and "weakness" paradigm. The new approach categorizes feedback as "continue" or to keep repeating a certain behavior, and "consider" or to think about changing something. Both approaches come from the world of coaching. Similar to the guidance versus feedback framework, this distinction helps employees focus on forward-looking, action-oriented changes, and casts feedback in a positive light.[30]

---

30 Leonardo Baldassarre and Brian Finken, "GE's Real-Time Performance Development," *HBR*, August 12, 2015.

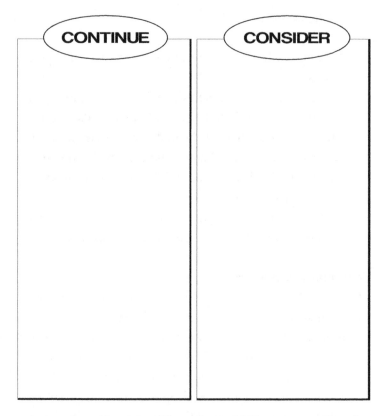

CONTINUE

CONSIDER

Instructions: List three things you would like to see continued, and one to two things you would like the person/teammate/ employee to consider doing differently.

Who can use this?

- One-on-one Leader to Direct Report and a Direct Report to a Leader
- Team—everyone completes one for everyone and you verbally share in three-to four-minute rounds, one-on-one with each other. At the end, you review all of the feedback and look for themes, taking away the top three

things you should continue and the top three things you should consider doing differently.

- Cross Functionally—this could work well in project teams following the steps above as a team as well.

THE AWKWARDNESS CONTINUES

Back to the embarrassing lettuce in braces saga! Do you say something or let it go? Three weeks later, I was meeting the CEO in Rhode Island for yet another meal—dinner. Before I opened the door to the restaurant, I looked at the reflection and said Brené Brown's mantra, "Don't shrink. Don't puff up. Just stand your sacred ground."[31]

We were catching up on some funny work-related stories over an appetizer and a glass of wine. I decided it was time. I started the conversation with, "Can I ask something that may be uncomfortable for you, and for me?" The smiled vanished, he turned serious, and said, "Nicole, absolutely!" I asked if he noticed anything in my braces when we ended lunch during our ninety-day plan discussion. Before I could get the question out of my mouth, he had turned bright red, and his head bowed down.

Time to lean into the discomfort and not run from it. I said, "That must have been really hard for you to see." He replied, "I am just not good at that stuff, you know, like the whole stain on your shirt." We both laughed for a short moment and I went on to say, "I understand it is uncomfortable. I have to know, how will I know you will be able give me honest,

---

31 Brené Brown, *The Gifts of Imperfection: Let Go of Who You Think You're Supposed to Be and Embrace Who You Are* (Center City: Hazelden Publishing, 2010), 107.

just-in-time feedback if you aren't able to tell me about something as trivial as this?"

I paused.

We both sat in silence at the power of the question in front of us.

I trusted silence even though my natural instinct was to let him off the hook.

.

.

.

Finally, he responded with, "I am sorry. I had not thought about it quite this way."

That evening over dinner, we began to lay out agreements for us both to be successful. Straight talk enabled us to open up powerful dialogue and shift our relationship to a much deeper level because we were aligned. He ended up being one of the best leaders I ever worked for. He wasn't perfect, but neither was I. We took the time to invest in our relationship and scope out how we wanted to work together to be successful.

You see, we always have the option.

We can remain silent or talk straight. Looking back, I can't imagine not speaking up. What would life have been like? My prediction is I would not have been successful. It would not have ended well. That moment of small bravery ended up being so transformational for me in that role.

This is a defining moment for you, me, all of us! When you know you need to talk straight and have not, ask yourself these questions:

☑ What is the story I am telling myself about the moment?
☑ What would best serve the work and the people?
☑ What is the bravest thing I can do right now? What is one move I can make or action I can take?

Brave Leaders have an intense desire for change. In other words, they don't accept things as they are. They instead want to always make things better, to always upgrade their life and circumstances.

5.

THE ART OF FAILING: SLIPS, TRIPS, AND FALLS

"The master has failed more times
than the beginner even tried."

—STEPHEN MCCRANIE

"Are you ready for me?" she asked as she stepped into my office. It was my new purchasing manager. My role was expanding from leading all of HR to now including purchasing and facilities, and this was our first official meeting. What I loved most about this manager was how her personality could fill a room. Yet here she was starting off our discussion in a quiet voice, saying, "We have a problem and I need your help." I matched her seriousness quickly and said, "Of course, what is going on?" She went on to say, "The CEO is signing the CRO's (chief risk officer's) expense reports." She held a long pause and finished by saying, "The CRO is also signing the CEO's expense reports."

We were a private company in the process of being acquired by a public company. If we didn't fix this, it would be an issue—a big issue. In the spirit of wanting to do the right thing, I suggested to the CEO we add a third person into the rotation: CEO signs for CRO, CRO signs for the CAO, and the CAO signs for the CEO. He listened, asked a few questions, and then moved on to a new topic. Naively I thought he would be on board with the recommendation. It was only a mere twenty-four hours later when our CAO (chief administrative officer) called me to let me know the CEO had requested him to tell me to stop and to not bring it up again.

I would come to learn this was just the beginning. His reaction to what seemed like a simple solution made me realize there was more to this, especially since he pulled a cowardly move and sent the CAO to deliver the message. I asked the purchasing manager to confidentially pull both of their expense reports for the past year and flag any areas of concerns. We would meet to review them when she was ready.

SLIPS, TRIPS, AND FALLS

Slips, trips, and falls can happen anywhere and can result in serious injuries or death. Millions of Americans seek medical treatment for falls and thousands more die from them every year. You can take steps to prevent slips, trips, and falls by being aware of hazards in your home, workplace, or other surroundings. Slips, trips, and falls are among the most frequently reported accidents in the United States.

Technically speaking, slips, trips, and falls are three separate things. Slips consist of situations in which you lose your footing and balance. Trips happen when you lose your balance because your foot, leg, or body hits a fixed object. Both can cause a fall. But falls can also happen because a support, such as a guardrail or handhold, fails or is missing. Falls can be the leading cause of death in working adults depending on the industry, according to OSHA's injury facts.[32]

I had the opportunity to lead many teams in corporate environments and manufacturing environments. As a leader, making sure everyone went home safely to their families every day or night was extremely important. Slips, trips, and falls were typically our number one recorded injury to OSHA. I started thinking about my own failures as slips, trips, and falls in degrees of severity in relation to my own failures as a leader.

---

32 Slips, Trips, and Falls, Occupational, Safety, and Health Association.

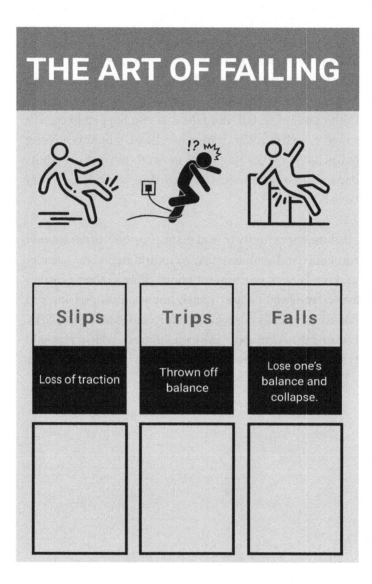

THE ART OF FAILING

Slips	Trips	Falls
Loss of traction	Thrown off balance	Lose one's balance and collapse.

SLIPS

I had just taken on a new role at Conagra Brands, which was then called Conagra Frozen Foods. I was transitioning to lead the human resources department, which included safety and training for one of their top manufacturing facilities. The site had just completed a survey on how human resources was performing in the facility. As I was reading through the results, and one comment seemed to echo many of the other complaints.

Going to HR for help is like getting an enema.

It wasn't good, and we had a lot of work to do. What I quickly realized as I was rolling up my sleeves, listening, and learning was many of them just didn't know what great looked like. They weren't clear on expectations and, in absence of those, created their own. They had no strategy, goals, or even operating norms. When the entire facility was expected to be there on a Saturday to do inventory, HR didn't show up. We were somehow exempt from the work but were kind enough to order pizzas for the facility.

Time to get to work setting strategies and creating goals for their first key performance indicators (KPI's), their metrics for success and operating norms. Operating norms are the rules and routines we want to ensure we deliver on our strategy and goals. For example, when the entire facility needs to be here, we are here. When the facility works twenty-four/seven, we do as well for coverage.

With about four years of leadership experience under my belt, I was a bit naive. The slips we made as a human resources team gave us the opportunity to be better and to grow in what we could deliver. Every chance I got, I would share with the team how we could recover from slips such as the comment about how going to human resources felt like an enema. It is about choice. Are we willing to hear what they have to say? Yes, and when we do, we regain our balance and deliver at a much higher level.

TRIPS

One morning, I was opening an email from a client. She had forwarded me a note from her CEO. It read, "Nicole is stirring the pot. Fire her."

Whoa! Fired? This was a big contract. What made it worse was this was new territory for me. In seven years of consulting and leadership development, I've never been fired, or even close to being fired.

I was thrown off balance for a bit. I didn't want to be fired. What would people say? Would being fired hurt my business? I didn't want my reputation to be hurt by this one event. I instantly wanted to beg for forgiveness and save the relationship at all cost.

My coach's voice rang in my head, "Hold on a second, Nicole! Take a deep breath." I replayed the conversations in my mind. I had collected data from his team and shared back with him the results, just like we had agreed. I simply held up the mirror to his current reality and he flat out didn't like it. He hired me to help make him and his leadership team be more effective, and what I learned in the process was he was a big part of the problem.

What I realized was the CEO had never received feedback like this before, not because he hadn't been behaving this way, but because nobody had been brave enough to share the feedback until now, at age fifty-five, to him. The plan of action we had designed was for a leader who was ready to accept the feedback and take immediate action. I was asking him to be vulnerable. I asked him if we could meet for lunch to talk. He said sure but wanted his chief administrative officer (CAO) to join. I quickly understood I had lost some trust there. We sat down for lunch, and I opened the conversation to let him know I was sorry and the direction we moved was likely aggressive for the situation, yet I knew he was capable of so much more.

He opened up and told me he felt like his pants had been pulled down.

He felt exposed. He didn't realize he was the issue. We spent much time at the lunch exploring what a path forward could look like. We continued our important work together back in balance and so much learned from that trip.

FALLS

My purchasing manager had pulled the expense reports and scheduled some time to discuss them. I could tell by the look on her face as she stepped into my office, it wasn't good. She had a large stack of expense reports with those little colored flags poking out. What I learned was the CEO and CRO were approving each other's extracurricular activities, which at that point were only personal lavish travel. I had been warned by the CEO through the CAO not to pursue this. This started as a trip and ended in a fall.

What I learned later changed everything. Their insatiable love of prostitutes and drugs drove their paranoia to an all-time high, ruling me as a potential threat to the company who recently acquired us. So, they convinced the parent company they would no longer need an executive level HR leader and to eliminate the position and me. What they did not know was I had no idea about the drugs and prostitutes at that point, no idea at all.

I didn't want to be fired or have my position eliminated, but there was a high likelihood I was going to be let go before the CEO and CRO got fired themselves. Once I had time to reflect on the whole experience from the beginning, I realized it really doesn't matter how hard you work, driving strategy, designing the best people practices, building a strong culture, or implementing leadership and executive development because it can all be gone in a moment. It was unsettling to me. The moment of almost being fired for doing the right thing made me pause and think about what I really wanted to do.

I remember an executive leadership strategy session I designed and facilitated in Providence, Rhode Island. We started off the evening before with cocktails and dinner, beginning the strategy work the next morning at nine o'clock. Everyone was there except the CRO. Several said, "Let's get started," laughing, knowing the CRO had too much to drink the night before. We started and almost an hour went by, but still there was no CRO. I paused and asked one of the leaders to go knock on his hotel door to make sure he was okay. Plus, you really can't have a strategy session without your CRO, especially one who was known to be an antagonist.

The leader who went to check on the CRO returned, letting us know the disheveled CRO was okay and would be down soon. He managed to bring himself down to the meeting. He looked like hell. Obviously, it was more than just a night of heavy drinking. Later, we learned the blow and hooker in his room were what prevented him from attending the strategy session on time. That's just how messed up this all was.

A brave leader knows it is okay to get fired once in a while, for the right reasons.

The executive leadership team saw what was about to go down, my "position elimination," and stepped in to stop it. Shortly following this move, the CEO, CRO, and a few other executives were fired for their many transgressions.

Have you ever started to fall and realized...

Oh crap, this is going to leave a mark.

It is happening, you are in the midst of falling, and there is just nothing you can do about it. You know you are going down hard and it's going to be painful. While I wasn't the one fired in this scenario, something snapped in me. I realized I had been giving 150 percent to a role at a company that didn't value me or my role in the same way. After I picked myself up, watching my bruises and cuts heal, I realized I needed to work at a company where I could lead transformation, make a difference, and stop playing small. The fall inspired me to do so much more.

TAKE A CHANCE

A chance is a possibility of something happening. When we take chances, we are experimenting and trying something new.

We don't realize it, but we take chances every day. Chances can be something small, like a new route to a favorite place, or trying a new place, or picking up the phone and calling someone you haven't connected with in a while. Taking chances can be bigger too, like writing this book and putting my voice out there in the world.

If we are intentional about taking chances, imagine the possibilities.

My dear friend Tasha shared during our Being Brave Series, "So one of the things I've been doing is setting aside time to write because I love to write, but I've never really blogged publicly. I set myself a goal that I was going to write every single day during shelter in place. So I did it. I did it for almost forty-five days. Then I let up, and now I'm kind of realizing I love it. I love doing a little daily vlog Monday through Friday. Speaking out allows me to take some of the experiences we've had and share it with my community. It also just gives me practice with the process of writing and putting out content. I think everyone's looking for content right now. I cannot tell you how nervous and worried I was in this beginning. I thought, what if I don't have anything to say? What if people don't like it? What if they have an opinion? Then I just realized that's not why I'm doing it. I'm doing it to be brave. So, that's one very specific action I took that I am so grateful for."

STEPPING INTO DISCOMFORT

It's more of these small, subtle opportunities that encourage us to step into our own discomfort.

This past year, I had the opportunity to interview Leah Vetter, area president at Gallagher. She is an incredible leader, driving strong results and investing in her own personal and professional growth. I asked her, "What is helping you be brave right now?" She paused and responded with the most powerful question:

> **I asked myself, "What if it was all meant for me, right now in this given moment, to show up in a different way and to learn and grow?"**

She paused. I paused. I was hanging on to her next words as she continued saying:

"So there is all of this—this pandemic, this uncertainty, being a leader in this time where there's this need for anti-racism and standing up and speaking out—right? By making that mind shift happen, I've allowed myself to think and look for the opportunities in it versus being reactive and thinking, oh my gosh, all this is happening to me. What can I do? Or how

am I going handle it? So, it kind of puts me in a position of being more proactive, versus just responsive or reactive. Why am I uncomfortable here? Share why you are uncomfortable and allow that to be a connection point with others. What if we appreciated the duality, this feeling of being incredibly insecure and yet confident in what we are doing?"

Being Brave is seeing the opportunity in all things. Leaders who practice small brave moves recognize the slips and trips are a part of the journey.

We think the journey should be straight line from point A to point B, and what it really looks like is:

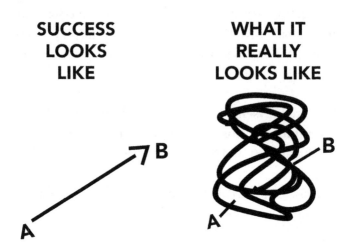

We have slips, a few trips, and maybe a fall to get there.

It also reminds me of The Messy Middle.[33]

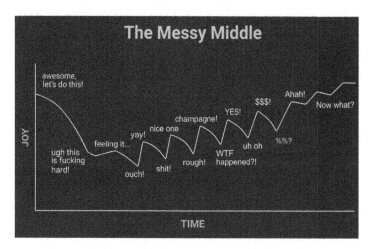

The Messy Middle by Scott Belsky

Brave Leaders accept every experience has some form of value and benefit for them. In other words, no matter what happens, they remain hopeful that in the end things will turn out in their favor.

Here's the thing: sometimes we have to reframe our past mistakes. Whether we like it or not, they aren't going anywhere. They are part of our fabric. They are our story. But they don't define us. Instead of trying to erase our past failures, let's focus on what they have taught us. Have they made us more compassionate, wiser, more understanding, or more grateful?

---

33   Scott Belsky, *The Messy Middle: Finding Your Way Through the Hardest and Most Crucial Part of Any Bold Venture* (New York: Penguin Random House, 2018), 5.

At Big Canvas Improv, founder Doug Rothgeb challenges leaders to think failure *is* an option. When we work with Doug and the improv team, we do an exercise with new leaders where they proudly shout "I failed" and take a bow. We all wildly clap and cheer them on. Celebrating our failures as leaders remind us it is okay and teaches us to move on.

Also, don't fake it 'til you make it. That's terrible advice.

Face it 'til you make it!

Get up. Work hard. Fail. Stand back up! Face it again. Do a little better. Fail again. Get back up.

Brave Leaders fail, get back up, and never stop trying.

6.

LEAN ON YOUR CIRCLE

"You cannot swim for new horizons until you have the courage to lose sight of the shore."

—WILLIAM FAULKNER

You don't have to go at this bravery thing alone. Bravery is infectious. Draw strength from friends, family, and colleagues. To be able to lean in, you have to lean on. A swim buddy is one of those people.

WHAT IS A SWIM BUDDY?

In truth, the buddy system is fairly simple. It's just what it sounds like. Swimmers, particularly children, should not swim alone. Even if you have a basic knowledge of how to prevent yourself from drowning, it cannot keep you totally safe. Taking a dip with another swimmer of similar swimming ability can greatly increase your safety. Even if a lifeguard is present, they are typically watching a large number of swimmers.

When I was a young teen, we vacationed for a week in Yankton, South Dakota. I do not remember much about this trip because I was at odds with my parents that summer. As a fourteen-year-old, I was demanding more independence and freedom and was always greeted with a, "Hell, no." I have a bit of a rebellious streak in me, so the more control they wanted, the more I wanted to do just the opposite.

My brothers Richie and Robbie, two family friends, and I were swimming in a large outdoor community pool. My brother and his friend decided to gang up on my little brother, Robbie, who was ten years old. If you were to place a bet this day, it would be on my little brother antagonizing them until they ultimately had to retaliate. You know, it was brothers being brothers.

Here they were in the deep end of this large, Olympic size pool when suddenly I heard my little brother screaming, "Coastguard! Coastguard! Coastguard!" Richie and his friend were playfully dunking him to make him pay for his antagonizations, and he was calling for the Coast Guard. Unfortunately, the Coast Guard doesn't patrol community pools. The lifeguard, who could not have been any older than eighteen, didn't relate "Coast Guard" to really meaning, "Lifeguard, help me!"

Cue me making a sister move—the middle child, the mediator, the interpreter, *me*. I splashed my way over to the lifeguard to get their attention, letting them know he is in fact calling for them and not the Coast Guard. Swim buddies always have your back. I would always be my little brother's swim buddy.

SWIM BUDDIES WILL TELL YOU THE TRUTH AND HOLD YOU ACCOUNTABLE.

The principles of the swim buddy apply 100 percent to us as leaders. Let me explain how. A swim buddy can be a close friend, spouse, colleague, or even a sibling who has been there for you during difficult times. A swim buddy holds you accountable and is not afraid to let you know you screwed up. A swim buddy is a sounding board during a crisis or life-changing event. At a minimum, when you call a swim buddy, they will answer the phone or get back with you fairly quickly.

Accountability is a huge part of developing a Bravership lifestyle. A swim buddy is there to hold you accountable. However, accountability works in both directions. By nature of the relationship, you are the swim buddy to your swim buddy. That means you have to be there for them just as much as they are there for you.

We were in the middle of a worldwide business transformation at Conagra Frozen Foods, and I was leading the people side of the transformation across our entire supply chain. This transformation required us to turn around the mediocre performance on many of our brands and facilities. Of equal importance, it was not just "what" we needed to deliver but "how" we delivered it. We had to shift the culture from one of grinding people, blaming and finger pointing, and a high level of turnover to a culture of working and winning together. I was tasked with designing and implementing people practices across our supply chain, enabling us to win together.

I was riding the corporate jet to do a tour of different plants with our Frozen Foods executive team, including our president Dean Hollis. He was sitting directly across from me on the jet, and as we began conversation for the journey, I asked how things were going for him. What I loved, and still do love, about Dean is his strong belief in radical transparency. He believes in it and models it. He went on to share with me how we were making progress, how he was pleased but not satisfied, and how everyone had to really get performance moving. He smiled as he shared how he had just watched the movie *Finding Nemo* the night before with his young children, and how that famous phrase resonated and landed.

Just keep swimming

Just keep swimming

Just keep swimming swimming swimming

What do we do we swim, swim, swim.

In the movie *Finding Nemo,* Dorie starts the scene with, "You know what you gotta do when life gets you down?"[34] Dean was right. We had to keep swimming. It was the only way we could accomplish what we needed to accomplish. We knew the transformation would be tough, and there would be good days, bad days, and other days.

---

34 Lee Unkrich, and Andrew Stanton, 2003, *Finding Nemo*, United States: Buena Vista Pictures.

"Curate your circle, put intentionally around you those people who make you better and who you can make better."

—LAURIE BAEDKE

YOUR CIRCLE OF SWIM BUDDIES SHOULD BE SMALL.

My daughter, Moe, recently shared with me a TEDx Talk she had been creating. A goal of hers is to take the stage! It is called "Creating the Ultimate A-Team."

She had been struggling with the friendship transition from high school to college. Friendships in your twenties can be challenging. You are not meeting as many people as you did in high school or early college, and you spend so much time trying to maintain those high school and early college relationships, only to find the efforts overwhelming and disappointing. You are trying to figure yourself out, while realizing you are changing and so are they. Do you hold on for history's sake or let go?

Moe took the time to reflect and determined it was simple. She just wanted to be a good friend. For her to do that, she had to downsize her "circle" of friends. She wrote down on a piece of paper her friends whom she loved unconditionally and her friends who loved her unconditionally—the inner circle, the most loving and mutual relationships. Guess how many people she wrote down? She wrote down six.

So much pressure is put on kids and teenagers to have tons of friends, especially girls, through means such as the BE KIND movement and being inclusive to all. You can be kind to everyone yet relieve yourself from the pressure of thinking you need to be friends with everyone. In doing so, you'll be able to focus your energy and attention on your actual close friends.

Moe made a small brave move that ended up having a big effect. She created her "A-team," which included six of her closest friends, with the goal to be the best possible friend she can be to those six people. This allows her to go deeper and have stronger and more fulfilling relationships. The six, unaware of the "A-Team," show up for her in return. She doesn't pretend to have it all right, and the beautiful part is she is learning, growing, and fostering intentional relationships. Those are her swim buddies.

As your life changes, so will your circle. You have to be willing to bring new people into your circle and bless and release the ones who no longer serve a purpose. This is called growth, which is a good thing.

"A swim buddy should be unselfishly fired up for you and want to be there during the successes and failures of your journey."

—DAVID RUTHERFORD

In many of our leadership programs, we intentionally design swim buddy experiences. It gives a leader someone to go deep with who is experiencing the program with them throughout the six to nine months. You choose your swim buddy. My challenge is often to the group of leaders to choose someone they don't work closely with. Early on, they spend one-on-one time with each other by using a list of questions to get to know each other better and quickly going deep. The expectation is they will be there to cheer each other on, pick each other up, talk straight, and act as a loving critic when needed throughout the program. Most times these swim buddies continue long after the program is complete.

YOUR TRIBE

Leadership presence expert and Amazon bestselling author of the *Bold New You and Unleashing Potential* Justin Patton shared what is helping him be braver within his tribe: the people with whom he chooses to surround himself. He shared his favorite quote of all time from Oprah:

> *Everyone in life just wants to know three things, they wanna know:*

Do you see me?

Do you hear me?

And does what I say mean anything to you at all?

Justin went on to say:

> *And for me, it's my tribe, that right now when it's been really difficult, has made me feel seen and heard. They've given me the space to vent and just talk about what I'm thinking and feeling without judgment and with empathy, which I really needed. They've given me*

resources when the economy tanked. They pushed me to think differently about my business and have been there to give me their ideas and review stuff for me. I even consider the people in my social media part of my tribe. I really am intentional about following people who inspire me or just make me laugh because I think that's all we need right now. I'm a big believer if you ever have to give up who you are for other people, then you're with the wrong people. It is important to say goodbye to people who no longer should be in your tribe. My tribe has been there for me when it was hard in the past and hard right now, and I know they will be there when it's hard in the future. So, my tribe is what makes me braver.

Justin played an important part in my journey back in 2012. We met while going through a leadership assessment certification and became fast friends. He is someone who pushes and challenges me to think bigger. I appreciate it.

Are we as intentional as we should be with whom we surround ourselves? Tony Robbins shares, "Proximity is Power. Always remember that who you spend the most time with is who you eventually become. To reach new heights of success, you must surround yourself with people who not only inspire you, but challenge you. It isn't always easy, but it's worth it."[35]

It is time to surround yourself with people who elevate you, who are already successful, and who push you outside of

---

35   Tony Robbins, "How to Surround Yourself with Good People: A Complete Guide," *tonyrobbins.com.*

your comfort zone. It takes small brave moves to do that. I was recently coaching an emerging leader who, through our coaching, uncovered the need to expand her internal network within her company. Once she identified the three leaders she wanted to begin networking with, the next step was to make the ask.

The courage to ask a leader to connect and serve as a mentor, advisor, or connector can be difficult. We tell ourselves stories like, "They are too busy, they won't have time for me," or, "I feel bad asking when I have nothing to give." Stop! They do have time for you! Most are waiting to be asked! The best leaders want to give back; it is a part of their legacy. They want to share their knowledge, experience, and cheer you on! You have to be willing to build your small circle with small brave moves.

EMBRACING MY CIRCLE

I love my circle and it evolves over time. If I am lucky, the good ones stay for decades. On October 13, 2006, I was at a conference in San Diego when I received a horrifying call. It was my dermatologist. She said I had cancer—melanoma. They had to get me scheduled for surgery immediately. I remember bursting into tears and hanging up the phone. This particular trip, Dave was with me. I left the conference and went back to the hotel to find him. He held me so tight with the most encouraging words he could find. I was scared of a death sentence. I didn't know how to lean on my circle.

My prognosis was good because we detected it early, but it would require a significant surgery. I remember my leader at the time, Al, offering to call the very best cancer specialists to get a second opinion and ensure we were eliminating any risk. I remember my friends showed up with meals and flowers. My mom would not leave my side for any of the appointments. I couldn't ask for help. I didn't know what to ask for. Yet they showed up and held me tight.

My bravest move? Opening the door to let them in—letting them see all of me.

Daniel Coyle talks about vulnerability and creating a sense of belonging in his book *The Culture Code*. He explains vulnerability doesn't come after trust, but precedes it. Leaping into the unknown, when done alongside others, causes the solid ground of trust to materialize beneath our feet. We must be willing to be vulnerable to invite our circle in and let them see us.[36]

I also believe sometimes swim buddies play a role just for a certain period of time, not forever, which is also okay. The ones who stick around and transition with your relationship as you both grow are the keepers. They are the ones you want by your side no matter what.

WHAT SHOULD YOU LOOK FOR IN A SWIM BUDDY?

---

36 Ibid.

Reflection

Attributes you would like in a swim buddy.

....

....

....

....

Characteristics that make you a good swim buddy.

....

....

....

....

List of people you consider your swim buddies.

＿＿＿＿＿＿＿＿＿＿＿＿＿＿＿＿＿＿＿＿

＿＿＿＿＿＿＿＿＿＿＿＿＿＿＿＿＿＿＿＿

＿＿＿＿＿＿＿＿＿＿＿＿＿＿＿＿＿＿＿＿

＿＿＿＿＿＿＿＿＿＿＿＿＿＿＿＿＿＿＿＿

Is there anyone you need to get rid of? I ask this because it is a tough question. And answering tough questions helps us gain clarity and move toward action one small brave move at a time.

*

*

*

It takes small brave moves to cultivate your crew. What if a small brave move is to introduce this concept to individuals who have not heard of it?

Remember, we were meant to face adversity with close friends who can count on us as much as we can count on them.

HABITS TO BUILD:

- Schedule regular check-ins
- Practice saying: Here's what I need from you right now.
- Practice asking: What do you need from me right now?

Brave Leaders build their circles, invest in their circle, and know what their circle gives back is priceless.

7.

BEING THERE
FOR OTHERS

———

Let people draw bravery from you. Helping
someone else be brave can help you be brave.

Colonel Gerry Schwartz had just pulled into the hotel parking lot where he and his team of weekend reservists would
be staying. He pulled in next to a young female barefoot
sergeant more than half out of uniform unloading her vehicle. Sitting in his Volvo with his window down, he uttered
the words, "Are you freaking kidding me?" At parade rest,
the army sergeant responded with, "I have no excuse." Her
"I have no excuse" was a response of despair and the feeling
of giving up.

The army has a set of standards for uniform and appearance where discipline is judged. Therefore, a neat and well-
groomed appearance by all soldiers is fundamental to the
army and contributes to an effective military force. A vital

ingredient of the army's strength and military effectiveness is pride and self-discipline. It was the day before the beginning of their two-week annual training as reservists. Colonel Schwartz served every day with an immense amount of pride. As the leader of his team, it was important for him to mentor and teach everyone on his team, holding them all to the high standards of the army.

What the colonel didn't know was how broken this young sergeant was in every aspect of her life.

"The army pontificates 'The Standard.' The standard is black and white. That is the expectation, but the reality is there is a spectrum. I learned the most loved, respected, and honored leaders in the army are the ones who take the time and invest the energy to care just a little and see their soldiers for the shades of gray that they are and nudge them whichever way necessary to move them forward in life and profession. There was no way he knew what was going on in my life when he gave me a chance to redeem myself or knew how much that would mean to me. But his leadership in that moment helped me to see that my world wasn't hopelessly full of monsters and dead ends."—A young female sergeant

Over the next two weeks, Colonel Schwartz would call on her by name, praising her for what she was doing right and not chiding her for all she did wrong. He continued to micro-check in with her throughout the annual training, never bringing back up the incident in the parking lot. The grace he gave her played a significant role in building up her self-esteem, which was at an all-time low.

"By knowing my name and calling upon me in a gigantic briefing, he provided me with an opportunity to demonstrate some kind of value."

He had lifted the pressure of feeling like a failure for a few days, a feeling she had learned to accept most of her life. She became excited and engaged in the training. The team was unified in a task where they felt purposeful and proud of their work. The team chose to embrace her, and they became her island oasis. Colonel Schwartz gave her room to feel forgiven, which allowed the opportunity for her to forgive herself, ultimately saving her life.

About a year later, Gerry was cleaning out his office. His thirty-year career with the army was coming abruptly to an end. He noticed on his desk a pile of cards from soldiers he had led throughout his career. It was already an emotional day for him as he opened the card laying at the top of the stack. He recognized the handwriting immediately and went back to the moment they had met. As he began to read the card, tears filled his eyes.

This young sergeant wrote how she had planned to end her life at the end of their two-week annual training but chose not too because Colonel Schwartz had seen something inside of her. She no longer felt invisible because of the interest he took in her. He was there for a young sergeant who needed something more.

Did he know all of the details of her story? No, he did not. As a leader, he showed up consistently for his entire team. As a result, he saved a life just by being there for her.

BEING THERE FOR OTHERS DEFINED

Be aware and notice someone may need you right now.

They can't ask in that moment.

Let others draw bravery from you.

No need to give advice, instead ask, "What's going on for you right now?"

Be available for emotional support, unconditionally, and without judgment.

This requires us to be aware of what is going on around us and pick up on what others might be trying to say.

Recently, I was coaching a female executive client who shared her next role was to assume her boss's role and ended the statement with, "I will be a disappointment." Wait, what? In that moment, I had a choice. I could have gone back over that statement or I could lean into her. I chose to lean in. I asked, "What's going on for you right now?" Being there for her and asking the question opened the path for a deep exploration, alignment, and ultimately an action for her to take.

Author Pam McLean shares in her book *Self as Coach, Self as Leader: Developing the Best in You to Develop the Best in Others* a concept I love called *turning up the heat*. She shares, "As leaders and coaches, the best thing we can do in being there for others is being willing to turn up the heat. What does that mean? Heat is a potent cauldron connecting head, heart, and gut in a mixture that creates an opening for meaningful breakthroughs—the sort that connect the dots, linking who we are today with our past, our narratives, our early attachments, and the scripts we crafted in our early years that no longer serve us as well in our current lives. Heat creates the possibility for new insights and epiphanies."[37] As coaches, we get the honor and opportunity to be there for our clients.

My friend was in the final days of saying goodbye to her father due to congestive heart failure. The hospital would only allow one visitor for one hour per day because we are in the middle of a pandemic. Her mom had been visiting every day for the past week or so. I asked, "So when are you going to go see your dad?" I was met with, "Mom is there every day, you know, and she likes to see him."

Me: "May I challenge you?"
Her: "Sure."
Me: "What would your dad want?"
Her: "Well, he would probably want to see me."
Me: "What do you want?"
Her: "Well, I want to see him too."
Me: "What is the real challenge for you?"
Her: "I am not good at this "feeling" stuff, I don't know what to say."

Now we are on to something. She wasn't sure what to say, how to act, or what to do during this visit, so we spent the next few minutes crafting what that could look like for her. The small brave moves she needed to make to see her dad. Having lost both of my parents, I wanted my friend to be able to look back with no regrets, whatever the outcome needed to be for her, no regrets.

---

37 Pamela McLean, *Self as Coach, Self as Leader: Developing the Best in You to Develop the Best in Others*, (Hoboken: John Wiley & Sons, 2019), 35–36.

LET PEOPLE DRAW BRAVERY FROM YOU.
In June 2020, I spoke with Mark Stelzner, founder and managing principle at IA, in my Being Brave series I launched right after COVID hit. He shared the following, "I've spent every week talking to C-suite leaders who just need a safe place to cry. What strikes me about that, which is super interesting, is it's not safe to be brave. It's not safe to be a leader of these organizations and to emote and to be human. I was talking to a senior HR executive of a large financial services firm, and he said, 'I've worked for this CEO for nine years and for the first time in my nine-year tenure and relationship with the CEO, he called me on my cellphone just to chat—just to catch up, just to see how I am. Just to check in.' So my hope is this is normalizing and humanizing all of us, and I think humbling many people that perhaps needed to be humbled. In a way that can create energy for whatever comes next."

Research has found many examples of how doing good, in ways big or small, not only *feels* good, but also *does* us good. For instance, the well-being-boosting and depression-lowering benefits of volunteering have been repeatedly documented, as has the sense of meaning and purpose that often accompanies altruistic behavior. Even when it comes to money, spending it on others predicts increases in happiness compared to spending it on ourselves. Moreover, there is now neural evidence from fMRI studies suggesting a link between generosity and happiness in the brain. For example, donating money to charitable organizations activates the same (mesolimbic) regions of the brain that respond to monetary rewards. In fact, the mere intent and commitment to generosity can stimulate neural change and make people happier.[38]

Nate Legrand, president and CEO of Center Point Financial Group, shared this with me just two months into the pandemic: "I try to make three calls a night to people, whether it's my grandparents, friends, relatives—people who might have fallen on hard times. I think right now what we're missing in a lot of ways is that interaction with people, and it's empowering for me to call them. How many people do you know that you say we're going to get together or talk at some point, and it never happens? I'm trying to do that, and again, it goes back to energy, and for me, that's helpful."

Reaching out to people who may or may not need you right now is a strong leadership habit to build.

Nearly twelve months into a global pandemic, many people are dealing with intense anxiety and depression under the pressures of isolation, prompting leaders to check in with their team, their peers, their friends, and family members on a regular basis.

Pandemic aside, it is a best practice for leaders.

YOUR PRESENCE IS THE INTERVENTION

I was coaching a C-suite executive in a Fortune 200 company. We had a six-month agreement for coaching. Amid heavy

---

38 Marianna Pogosyan, PhD, "In Helping Others You Help Yourself," *Psychology Today*, May 30, 2018.

transformation, her goal was to figure out how to bring others along with her.

All leaders face challenges and roadblocks. Some of these obstacles and difficulties stem from managing direct reports effectively, being able to prioritize conflicting responsibilities or the desire to keep growing with an organization. Even the best leaders use coaches to help them continue to develop their skills, self-awareness, and influence. A coach is a thought partner who can help you navigate issues, uncover blind spots, and identify opportunities for development.

Coaching is distinct from giving advice, consulting, counseling, or mentoring. You would hire a coach to help you with personal and professional goals, projects, or transitions. Your coach will help you grow by analyzing your current situation and identifying limiting beliefs and other potential challenges or obstacles you face. Then your coach will create a custom plan of action designed to help you achieve specific outcomes in your life.

After our third session, we were not moving toward action, not even one small step. At the end of our conversation, I raised my concern to her. She paused and reflected for a moment and told me how beneficial our coaching conversations have been for her. She also told me how she doesn't have time to process the massive transformation and turmoil it is causing on her team with anyone but me. While she may not have an immediate move she wants to make in our conversation, she is reflecting and making them as a result of our conversations. It was a reminder that leadership is a journey, and at different points we need different things. Right then, my presence was the intervention. Small brave moves would come as a result.

YOUR PRESENCE CREATES THE SPACE FOR LISTENING

It's impossible to truly listen to someone else when you're full of your own thoughts. That's why presence is the key to listening to other people. If you want to understand what someone else is saying, you need to be so present with them that you're taking in everything they're saying without filtering it through your own understanding. You need to be empty.

Imagine that between any two people having a conversation, they each have a giant basket full of their own beliefs, ideas, opinions, and experiences. Each time one person says something, their expression has to go into the other person's basket where it gets filtered according to their own worldview. To really be there for someone else, your basket has to be empty. I remind myself, basket empty and cup full.

BEING THERE FOR OTHERS IN ACTION

In a recent interview with Danielle Kirgan, chief transformation and human resources officer for Macy's, Inc., we talked about what being there for others really means during a pandemic.

"The concept of 'bravership' is brilliant. I see the concept *every* day in my own experiences in my leadership role that involves coaching and organizational effectiveness."

Kirgan shared she is in an industry under enormous pressure to evolve. The toughest decision in her career was when Macy's stores were designated as nonessential by government mandates in March 2020 and had to furlough 108,000 people. This sudden jolt forced the company into survival mode. They needed to conserve cash and make fast decisions. They also needed to lead with empathy and compassion for the 108,000 people—about 90 percent of our workforce—learning they would have no paycheck effective immediately.

They weren't alone though. I was coaching a chief medical officer who had to furlough ten of his team members deemed "nonessential." The CMO was struggling with how to explain to these PhDs, who were conducting important research to cure various diseases including cancer, that they were deemed "nonessential."

Macy's was forced to close for ten weeks, and yet, many of their competitors were allowed to operate. Kirgan went on to say:

"It calls for moments of panic, which are then balanced by flashes of 'bravership.' No one can teach or train you for these moments, but you pray you get it right. It is through the small brave moves that you practice. Then one day, you realize you've been preparing yourself and those around you for when you have to have big moments of bravery."

Kirgan was surrounded by pressure and feeling completely alone. She shared that when she feels overwhelmed with complexity, she leans into an important habit, which is writing it out.

She answers a series of questions including:

- What is the situation?
- What is the worst that could happen if we screw this up?
- How can we take care of others?
- How do we meet people where they are?

Kirgan shared she believes there is a solution for everything and finding out the solution needed to be her focus.

"We knew we weren't going to make everyone happy. We were brutally transparent with our decision sharing: here is what is happening, here is what we considered, here is the route we are going to take, and here is how we feel about it—we hate it."

Months later, I asked her about the impact of those decisions. What were employees saying?

Almost a year later, in March 2021, everyone has turned the page to focus on business growth.

In August 2020, just weeks after returning everyone back from furlough, Kirgan decided to do a pulse survey. Why? She wanted to know how they were doing. The pulse survey had the highest level of participation and the highest level of engagement results in recent years.

The transparency, how they communicated, and consistency of messaging had made a significant impact during an extremely hard time.

They repeated the pulse survey in January 2021 only to find an even higher level of participation and engagement. In addition, voluntary turnover is the lowest it has ever been in the past three years.

"Why do I get so emotional about my work? I care about the people."

Being a leader, you have people counting on you. Putting others first and taking care of others is important. Kirgan says, "I have to focus on our business winning in order to keep one hundred thousand employees."

BRAVE LEADERS ARE THERE FOR OTHERS

1. Just be there and listen. Your presence is the intervention. Sometimes keeping someone company while they go through their trials is a gift in and of itself.
2. Empathize with the other person's situation. Try, "You are in a tough situation," "Sounds like you're between a rock and a hard place," or, "I'm so sorry you have to face this kind of problem right now."
3. Tell a story. Instead of giving direct advice, tell a brief story about what happened to you or someone else (without violating anyone's confidentiality) that could shed light on their situation. Ask "May I share a story

about..." As Emily Dickinson wrote, "Tell the truth but tell it slant."[39] But don't make your story so long that you steal the spotlight from your friend.

4. Expand their perspective. If they are experiencing tunnel vision, help them expand their perspective. You could say, "Can I challenge your thinking here?" or, "Is there another way to look at this?" You could also expand perspective by pointing out the consequences of their actions to their future self: "This may seem like a good idea at this moment, but how will you feel in a week? A month? A year?"

5. Ask, "What is really important to you?" and other identity questions like, "What does no regrets look like in this scenario?" Identity questions help get in touch with the values that make them the person they are.

6. Ask, "How can I help?" Be prepared to set boundaries if direct help would draw you too tightly into their problem.

7. If you feel compelled to give direct advice, do it. Some truly want and need to hear your opinion. Straight talk, even when it may be hard to hear, can be just what they need.

Brave Leaders always focus on being generous and giving. They clearly understand by giving to others and by helping people overcome their problems, this allows them a greater depth of understanding about their own personal struggles. They consistently seek out opportunities to help and support. They understand only with other people's help will they have a chance of getting what they want.

---

39 Emily Dickinson and Martha Dickinson Bianchi, *The Complete Poems of Emily Dickinson: With an Introduction* (Boston: Little, Brown and Company, 1927), 236.

8.

BEING INTENTIONAL

———

*"Life should not be a journey to the grave with
the intention of arriving safely in a pretty and
well-preserved body, but rather an intention
to skid in broadside in a cloud of smoke,
thoroughly used up, totally worn out, bloodied
and loudly proclaiming 'Wow! What a Ride!'"*

—HUNTER S. THOMPSON

I opened the leadership session with, "When was the last
time you were intentional, and I mean really intentional?"

This program was designed for only twenty handpicked,
up-and-coming rock star leaders in a Fortune 500 company.
This seven-month program was brilliantly designed to ready
these rising stars for their next roles in the C-suite and was
only offered annually. We had the opportunity to be a small
part of their journey. The caliber of talent in the room suggested I would get a response of mockery given their results

and accomplishments. They knew me well enough to know I was being intentional about where I was heading with this, after all this was their final week of the program.

Intention is the essential process that precedes all our actions. We may not act on all our intentions, and "the road to hell *is* paved with good intentions." But we cannot act without them. Without intention, you likely would not be here reading this book. Our intentions can be weak, such as intending to drive to work and the car seemingly driving itself, finding ourselves there, and remembering almost nothing about the drive. Our intentions may be superhumanly powerful, like the intention of a mother lifting a truck off her injured child. If our intentions are unconscious and weak, our actions and our results will be weak. If our intentions are conscious and powerful, our actions and our results will be powerful.

But in all cases, we control our behavior and our results by controlling our intentions. We are the boss of our intentions. We are at perfect liberty to dial them up or dial them down. But our actions and the results we get will never be more powerful than our intentions. We are going to run an experiment on the power of intentions. I shared with the leaders that they are the scientists and the guinea pigs.

I asked the leaders to think of something they've wanted (or needed) to do for a long time—something that seems difficult to do, if not impossible, something they may have postponed several times or are outright procrastinating on accomplishing.

It will be an action that, if taken, could have powerful results for them and/or someone else. This is an action they could take today, in fact in the next hour, if their intention is strong enough. They had fifteen to twenty minutes to come up with their idea, starting now.

If they were confident they'd succeed, they probably chose something too easy. If they could imagine needing to summon more courage, needing to marshal more resources, and needing more than an hour, then they were on the right track. The point was they had one hour to skid in broadside in a cloud of smoke, used up and worn out, proclaiming, "What a ride."

I told them not to be overly concerned with succeeding—be concerned with staying intentional. If they hit an obstacle, go back to their intention and go again, and again, and again.

I told them to think about the thing they wanted to accomplish and the level of intention they had. Next, I encouraged them to imagine increasing that level of intention by double, then imagine doubling that amount of intention again. Now double it again.

Me: "Any questions before we start?"
One of the leaders raised their hand.

Leader: "Listen, we are all type A people. When we need to do something, we do it."
Leaning into the tension, I said, "I want you to think about something you have wanted to do. Something that feels too difficult, too hard, or you can't seem to find the time. You

have been given a gift today. Dig deep and seize the moment." Then they were off to think. I knew they weren't getting it just yet, but they would soon.

In January 2021, Cal Newport, author of *Deep Work,* shared his philosophy around focus and intentionality during our author call. He said, "Short sprints and deep work: the activities performed in a state of distraction-free concentration that push your cognitive capabilities to their limit. These efforts create new value and improve your skill and are hard to replicate."

Being Intentional Defined

What does it mean to be intentional? It means you have a clear purpose and are determined to act on the thoughts and feelings that are most important to you. When you embrace a mindset of intentional focus, you choose to live and create a life that has a clear purpose and is meaningful and exciting to you. Living with intention means you consciously choose to create the life you want, rather than having life, or other people, dictate your feelings and actions.

Dr. Mark Williamson, the director of Action for Happiness, and Professor Renata Salecl, a sociologist and philosopher, surveyed three thousand people in which 96 percent of them admitted living on autopilot.[40]

The year was 2008, I was starting my coaching certification program at the Hudson Institute of Coaching, and a part of

---

40   Mark Williamson and Renata Saleci, *Autopilot* (whitepaper).

the pre-program was attending and experiencing a program called Life Forward. This was a four-day signature experience to press "pause" in our busy lives and gain a broad view of our life path, exploring how life has unfolded up until now and contemplating how we would like to consciously shift and reshape elements of life going forward. The goal was to experience it firsthand so we could effectively coach our clients through their chapters and transitions. I was *all in!*

On day three, we began to create a vision board for ourselves. Designing the lives we wanted to shift toward was a very creative exercise. The process challenged us to create big goals for ourselves and think about what would need to be true to make it happen. This was the first time I had put down on paper a goal of starting my own business. Putting it down on this board made it more real than ever before. It would be a bold move for me at age thirty-seven as a wife, a mom to three young children, and with the weight of bringing the higher income into our family. Yet here I was putting it down. I had no idea what this business would exactly look like. I had a few scenarios in my mind. I remember writing down we would be the best at it. I filled the page with all my dreams, hopes, and aspirations.

Go big, I thought! I graduated from the coaching program in December of 2008 with my certification after an intense twelve months, 125 hours of training, one hundred hours of coaching, and one tough test. With the experience under my belt, I was ready to go.

Leaders who make small brave moves consistently take proactive action in the direction of their goals and objectives. In other words, they work hard and are intentional to ensure that things get better.

THE LETTER

Every year Greg Harris, CEO of Quantum Workplace, crafts a letter to all associates and key stakeholders at Quantum Workplace. The letter is deep in reflection about the past year's wins and losses, successes and failures. He opens up in his letter about his leadership wins and losses, successes and failures.

In our conversation, Greg shared more about this letter, FutureCast, that he first developed in 2006.

Me: "I have heard much about your annual letter. Why did you create this letter?"

Greg: "Why? To be intentional, solidify, and crystalize my own thinking. As CEOs, we tend to have a strategic attention deficit disorder, to be driven in our thinking and decisions by whatever worked today or yesterday and to then extrapolate that to the future, creating whiplash the larger our organizations gets."

Harris shared the letter is really 75 percent for him and 25 percent for the stakeholders. "To reflect and think about the times they took a swing and missed or didn't act quickly enough because we were waiting on more data. My optimistic goggles can get the best of me sometimes."

Greg went on to say, "For everyone to know, the more honest we are about when we make a mistake, the quicker we can correct it. The goal is to inspire us to be even better the following year and create a culture of psychological safety in making a mistake." He has asked, over the years, to his team, "Is it still relevant? Is it worth it?" His team provided a resounding, "Yes!" This letter is an opportunity to tamp down the noise and pull out the two to three most important lessons learned they should focus on.

Harris's vulnerability and authenticity are clear in how he intentionally wants to lead. These small brave moves he makes and models for his organization give permission for others to do the same.

SMALL BRAVE MOVES TO BE INTENTIONAL

1. Own Your Growth

Sometimes it's easier to close your office door and bury yourself in deadlines and commitments. One of the hardest challenges is breaking away from being a one person show and understanding the importance of building yourself and a stronger team.

To continue to develop as a good leader, engaging in continuous professional development is important. It not only helps to secure the professional position you are in, but it also leaves you with plenty of marketable skills for your professional future.

This could include formal training and education, work and life experience, or self-discovery and self-work practices. But don't limit yourself to just these options, seek professional development wherever and whenever you can.

2. Add Value

We should constantly be thinking of how we can add value to other people we interact with. This can be as simple as studying, understanding what drives them, and what they are passionate about. After you think of ways you can add value, you have to start looking for the opportunities in which you can add value to a person's life. Make them feel like their role in your life has a purpose that you welcome and value.

3. Become focused on your goals

One of the best ways to achieve a result that's important to you is to be intentional up front. The perfect framework for being intentional about what you want is to set goals, powerful goals. Goal setting gives you a plan and path to work toward every day and helps you start your day with intention. For goal setting to really work, you need to be emotionally and intellectually engaged in the result you want. This investment amplifies intentionality. You know why you want to achieve the goals, what specifically you want to achieve, and when you want to achieve it by. This clarity helps you set up each day with a clear knowledge of exactly what you want to do and where you want to invest your time and energy.

In 2014, in a column titled "The Art of Focus," David Brooks endorsed this approach of letting ambitious goals drive focused behavior explaining: "If you want to win the war for attention, don't try to say 'no' to the trivial distractions you find on the information smorgasbord; try to say 'yes' to the subject that arouses a terrifying longing, and then let the terrifying longing crowd out everything else."[41]

4. Time Blocking/Deep Work Scheduling

You need to dedicate yourself to a certain block of time to do something and don't try to overdo it. Just get done what you can in your amount of time. Video meetings can be just as productive in many cases and don't require as much time as physically going somewhere. So be mindful about guarding your time. Your ritual will need rules and processes to keep your efforts structured.

Much of my deep work occurred down at our little cottage on a lake about one and a half hours away from our home. It was my sanctuary; overlooking a body of water was inspiring and refreshing, and the ideas flowed. I could center, unplug, and allow the deep work to unfold. Each visit included an evening to gather with a small group of incredible friends. Downtime aids insights and helps recharge the energy needed to work deeply. The balance kept me going.

5. Create Accountability for Yourself

Share your intentionality with others.

While finishing this book, Eric Koester from the Creators Institute shared with me the phrase, "I have a big deadline with my publisher." He said by expressing it, I would create my own accountability for those closest to me. He was right. I used it to politely say "no" to things popping up as

---

41 David Brooks, "The Art of Focus," *New York Times*, June 3, 2014.

distractions. I regularly had others then asking, "How is the book going? Aren't you supposed to be working on your book?"

"A good intention clothes itself with power."

—RALPH WALDO EMERSON

Back to the leadership program and leading intentionally. After about ten minutes, leaders were ready to share what they wanted to accomplish in one hour. The first leader, Percy, said he wanted to learn to write music and play the guitar. He would research starting guitar lessons and get signed up within the hour. I responded with, "No, not big enough, write your first song and perform it for us, even just the first minute or two." He looked back at me. His expression changing from a smile to pure shock. I laughed and said, "You've got this, make it happen," and walked away. He may not have known he had it in him, but I did.

Another leader walked up. She wanted to investigate community service for her team. She shared they had been talking about it for the past six months but just haven't found the time to do it. She had moved almost a year ago to Portland to lead this team. I paused and asked, "What else?"

I trusted silence, and she took a deep breath and said, "Well, my mom," I could hear the quiver in her voice and I thought, we are getting closer. She went on to say, "She lives here, in Omaha, and is living in a senior care center. She has dementia and her condition is worsening. I thought I would be able to see her more when we come back for our leadership sessions, but most times our schedules are from early in the morning 'til late in the evening. It doesn't allow for me to leave and I don't have a car to go see her." I asked, "What would be the best use of your time for the next sixty minutes?" She hesitantly said, "To go see my mom." I said, "Okay, I am grabbing the keys to my car. I will see you in ninety minutes," giving her a little extra time for the trip. She had tears streaming down her face as she asked, "Are you sure?" I could not have been more certain about my decision. She had made tremendous sacrifices for this program. The time had come for her to do this.

A leader who I really was drawn to because of her story of perseverance pulled me aside to share how her mother had never met her three-year-old daughter because of issues in their relationship. She was going to FaceTime her mom, have a conversation, and then FaceTime her mom and daughter together to introduce them to each other.

A leader wanted to plan his and his wife's honeymoon. They were married ten years ago, moved with the company shortly after, and never had a honeymoon. He was going to plan it and surprise her.

I could share story after story of moments that would make your heart race in amazement or tears well up in your eyes. These leaders are incredible and were just beginning to understand the power of intention as we gathered back to share stories of what they accomplished in the past hour.

There is more inside of you than you know.
Brave Leaders are intentional.

9.

RELENTLESS CURIOSITY

"The urge to know is a powerful force. It keeps us moving forward, exploring, experimenting, and opening new doors."

—BRAVIUM HD

They said it could not be done.

It was a legacy union contract for the Teamsters, one that Jimmy Hoffa, the notorious leader of the International Brotherhood of Teamsters, himself had put together. The Teamsters were adamant. You don't ever break up legacy contracts.

Wait, there's more.

It was a dual contract with the United Food and Commercial Workers (UFCW) and the Teamsters.

One Company, Conagra Brands

Eight Manufacturing Sites

Two Unions

Ready for another layer of complexity? Conagra needed us to break up the contract so we could sell some of the plants to Pilgrim's Pride. Conagra wanted out of the chicken processing part of the business. Neither Pilgrim's Pride nor Conagra wanted to be in this messy contract together.

Ken, the chief negotiator, brought me in to be his lead negotiator, his right hand. As the new kid, at thirty-one years old, I was eager to get started. I immediately tried to figure out quick wins and ways to be successful. My naiveness was shining bright. Our first meeting with the Teamsters and the UFCW was in a dark dumpy hotel conference room in Arkansas. I was sitting across from George, the chief negotiator for the Teamsters. He was only fifty-five years old but looked much closer to seventy. He was staring me down while chain smoking. Yes, it was a little intimidating.

I had read the collective bargaining agreement and the countless memorandums of understanding. I was ready. Well, I thought I was ready. I went in trying to be an expert negotiator versus asking questions and learning. George responded to me with a deep stare and proceeded to ash his cigarette into my water glass. Damn, so much to learn.

When we are curious, we view tough situations more creatively.

In 2019, Landec appointed Dr. Albert D. Bolles as CEO to focus on operational excellence and profitable growth for the diversified health and wellness solution company. Al is a leader who is known to be an expert in many areas including leading with curiosity. He and I sat down to chat more about leveraging curiosity to be a braver leader.

"People come in with set points of view. It takes energy to keep asking questions. I have been burned by accepting the answer and moving on before, by not asking enough questions. To be a braver leader, we have to be the devil's advocate and make others work to show they have done the work behind decisions. Our decisions sometimes don't account for what is best for the customer or consumer. I was challenging my team about a packaging design once. The team was adamant we could not do the new bag design because of the cost and time. We knew it would benefit the consumer but were stuck. I had to bring in outside expertise to challenge our thinking and help us figure out a way to do it for a fraction of the cost and time."

We have to be willing to ask a tough question, and another, and another…

We were infusing new talent into the research and development side of our business at Conagra Foods back in 2006, and also centralizing the entire function under one leader, which was a massive transformation at the time. We needed to hire a new leader to help us drive innovation and shift the culture from a leader who would command and control, yell, scream, and berate while hopped up on Diet Coke to one of innovation and teamwork. Together, the new leader, Dr.

Albert D. Bolles, and I would begin to build the new centralized organization. I was this new leader's senior director, human resources business partner, and together we would begin transforming the business and the culture.

Part of the transformation included developing new technical and leadership competencies for the new Research, Quality, and Innovation organization.

"Nicole, as we are hiring food scientists, I want *curious chewers with hustle*," said Al. What he was describing was a mindset of people who can figure it out, ask great questions, chew on the responses, and then hustle to make something happen. He didn't want people who felt they were the only ones with the answers or people who would overanalyze decisions. He also didn't want us as leaders of his team to have all of the answers because how could we lead curious chewers with hustle?

Instead, he expected us to have friends in technical places. If it didn't work out the first time, you'd be curious, and you'd figure it out. You didn't have to have all of the answers, you just needed to have friends in technical places who could help you figure it out. First, chew on the problem by asking yourself how we can make it work. Then hustling to look at the external trends and get ahead of them.

"Holding a curious mindset is a great starting point when you're leading your team or organization. If you're in a truly new space, you won't always know the answers. Your team won't either. You're going to venture into the unknown together. Curiosity is a great way to lead that charge."—Tim Brown, CEO of IDEO

IDEO is known as early leaders of human-centered design, keeping people at the center of their work. It's a key tenet of design thinking and even as their methods evolve in response to new, complex challenges, they are always designing solutions for people first.

RELENTLESS CURIOSITY DEFINED

The term "curiosity" describes the intense desire to learn something. Relentless curiosity takes an individual's basic curiosity one step further. In fact, relentlessly curious people do not stop learning with the first explanation. When individuals are relentlessly curious, they are not content with yesterday's knowledge. They seek to understand.

A COACHING MINDSET

Leading as a coach who's interested in transformation and leading through change, knows how to point employees toward innovation and new experiences. To be a better coach, we have to be patient with the self-discovery approach, and it requires us to be relentlessly curious. According to *Chief Learning Officer,* effective coaches understand how to listen at a deeper level.[42] What would happen if your team felt you were really listening to them? It doesn't mean you have to grant wishes or let the inmates run the asylum. But hearing

---

42   Chris Westfall, "See What Happens When Leaders Listen," Chief Learning Officer - CLO Media, September 27, 2018.

other viewpoints can shape your own, as well as impact the effectiveness of the entire organization. You need to process without judgment and create a safe environment for new ideas.

Directing employees is a necessary part of managing. Leading creates freedom. When coaching is done correctly, there is greater freedom for the leader and greater empowerment for the employee. Motivation—the desire to do anything—only comes from one place and that is inside. To really change behavior and inspire new efficiency, focus your attention on where that drive really comes from, and you will be coaching yourself (and your team) to greater results.

Being "curious about what could be" has led me to open my ears and my mind to really listen to my clients to learn what is going on with them. It has caused me to be more open to learning and growing in each conversation. Being curious has made me more hopeful. It has made me more excited for my clients and their outcome and my listening has improved dramatically because of my curiosity.

What's different about listening from a curiosity mindset?

- I am able to fully listen without the distraction of "figuring it out" for my clients.
- I can listen more deeply to the said and unsaid when I'm genuinely curious about what's coming next.
- I am able to ask better questions, which enables them to arrive at better solutions for themselves.

GROWING YOUR CURIOSITY

We had only nine months to negotiate a successful union contract, and we were gone for weeks and even months at a time. The experience was similar to an accelerated MBA in leadership, influencing, and negotiations.

Here is what I learned:

- First, have a heart-to-heart with yourself about your ego. A good dose of humility goes a long way to giving up your sense of certainty about everything. You don't have to have all of the answers. We think we do, but we do not.
- Next, be a learner. When you genuinely want to learn something new, your curiosity will kick into overdrive.
- Constantly ask yourself, "I wonder…"
    - I wonder, what can I learn today?
    - I wonder, where could I go with this?
    - I wonder, what can I learn from this?
- Finally, frame problems as questions:

    ☑ What if?
    ☑ How might we?
    ☑ What could be possible?
    ☑ What is the situation?
    ☑ What is the challenge?
    ☑ What are possible solutions?

You must be willing to step outside of your comfort zone to be curious. We often surround ourselves with like-minded thinkers. Why? We draw energy from them, and it is just easier. Think about who you go to for insight, inspiration, and answers. Who do you engage with? Do you invite naysayers in or outside perspectives in?

I once worked for a leader who said to me:

"My job is to come up with the ideas, and Nicole, your job is write them down."

Being the expert in the room was always important to her. She had been my leader for almost eighteen months, and at this point she didn't take time to know me well enough to know one of my strongest thinking preferences was creativity and imagination. We don't have all the answers. It's okay not to be the smartest person in the room. It's okay not to have all the answers. Give ourselves permission not to be the expert all the time.

ADOPT A BEGINNER'S MINDSET

Expertise and experience are valuable assets but can be roadblocks. Approaching a challenge with fresh eyes can be a game changer. Consider the story of the Polaroid Instant Camera. The idea came when the founder's four-year-old daughter asked <u>one simple question</u>: *Why do we have to wait for photos?*

As you work on your own projects, keep asking *why*—especially when you think you know the answer.

We can learn a lot from children because they hold a beginner's mindset. I was talking with Mark Stelzner, founder and manager principal at IA, and he shared a story of his six-year-old, Jax. He told me about how Jax consumes voraciously any form of media and information and is constantly challenging through interrogative questioning. Simply put, Jax asks questions, challenging his parents. Mark went on to say, "What I see in him and what I love to see in others is a relentless curiosity, a tremendous amount of positivity and just the kindness and empathy that is really core to a child I think."

THE MARSHMALLOW CHALLENGE

I attended a leadership course early in my career at Center for Creative Leadership (CCL), and one of the exercises they put us through was The Marshmallow Challenge. The challenge, if you don't know, is a fun and instructive design exercise that encourages teams to experience simple but profound lessons in collaboration, innovation, and creativity. The challenge seems simple enough: small teams must build a structure in eighteen minutes using twenty sticks of spaghetti, one yard of tape, one yard of string, and one marshmallow. The winning team is the one who can construct the tallest free-standing structure with the marshmallow on top within the time allowed. The point of the exercise is to collaborate very quickly to respond to the task. It reveals some surprising lessons about the nature of collaboration.

The leaders spend a little time getting their heads around the task, jockeying for power, then laying out the materials and talking through the approach (the planning stage).

Then we spent most of the remaining time taping spaghetti together and wrapping string around arbitrary bits of the structure (the build stage). Then, with seconds to spare, someone grabbed the marshmallow and popped it on top of our structure. Needless to say, it fell over! My competitive team was not happy with our result.

The challenge has been done hundreds of times and the results are intriguing.

- **Who performs poorly?** Leaders. Why? They roll up their sleeves, competing with each other to get it done. They try to find the single correct plan and then attempt to execute that. They run out of time, and when they put the marshmallow on top, it's a crisis. Sound familiar?
- **Who performs well?** Kids. Why? First of all, none of the kids spend time trying to become CEO or leader of the group. More importantly, they start with the marshmallow and then build successive prototypes, all the time keeping the marshmallow on top until they find a solution that works.

They adopt an iterative, collaborative process and get instant feedback on what does and doesn't work. They are asking questions and being curious!

Brave Leaders approach everything with a sense of curiosity. They are curious about life and about the world around them. Given this, they are constantly in the act of exploring and experimenting in an effort to make things better.

When we demonstrate curiosity about others by asking questions, people like us *more* and view us as *more* competent, and the heightened trust makes our relationships more interesting and intimate. By asking questions, we promote more meaningful connections and more creative outcomes.

WHAT IF...

My friend, Shannon, introduced me to someone she thought would be a good fit for my business. When you own your own business, it is common to get referrals from friends or someone looking for a new role. Few really know and understand the work that goes into running a start-up. I have always been curious and held a lens in meeting with others of "how could they help grow the business?" and most times the conversation ended with disappointment. I was clear on the type of talent I wanted to expand and grow with. Maybe the bar was too high, but as the owner, you have to protect everything you have worked so hard to build.

She introduced me to Jeff Shannon. We had worked at the same company during a period of time and had never worked together, we only knew of each other. As I always did, I scheduled time to connect, and we agreed to meet over coffee. Regardless of how many of these conversations I have had, I always approached each one with a fresh mindset, curious to learn about this person and understand what their aspirations were. I left my conversation with Jeff intrigued and excited. He suggested we do something together, try it out.

About a week later I had a client who was looking for a workshop on innovation, right in Jeff's area of expertise. I made the call and he said *yes*! There we were at a two-day workshop for an up-and-coming e-commerce company. I led during day one and Jeff led day two.

As he was wrapping up day two of the workshop, I began to wonder what it might look like to do more together. What could the possibilities look like? He ended our session with the client sharing a powerful story around transformation and a butterfly. Did I mention butterfly? We took the next year to begin to build something we both had dreamed about.

The rest is history.

Dream big dreams and set your imagination loose on behalf of your clients. Don't limit their solutions to only those things within your understanding. We love surprising our clients with edgy ideas on how to deliver learning solutions. We know for transformation to happen, we have to be transformational.

THEY SAID IT COULDN'T BE DONE.

Ken and I went back to the caucus room filled with plant managers, plant human resources managers, and our legal team to plan our next moves. But first, Ken always pulled me aside and broke down what had just happened and why, enabling me to learn and grow. He taught me to ask questions, be curious, and slow down. The stakes were high, very high. His leadership throughout the process was a series of learning moments for me. I watched him nurture each union relationship carefully—how he led the caucus room, how he advised our executive leadership team at Conagra Frozen

Foods, and how he took time to prepare me for each discussion and debriefed every conversation.

Every step was done with relentless curiosity.

10.

EMBRACING UNCERTAINTY

"Challenges are gifts that force us to search
for a new center of gravity. Don't fight
them. Just find a new way to stand."

—OPRAH WINFREY

I jumped in the front seat of my dad's 1973 semi-tractor trailer truck that my dad used as a grain hauler for his farming operation. As he was going through a few of the important features, my mind was racing, and I could feel my heart beating out of my chest. Here was this farmer's daughter, born and raised on a farm yet had never driven any of the farming equipment. Why? Well, being the only girl with two brothers, my responsibilities were relegated to less skilled heavy labor.

While my brothers were behind the wheel of all of the expensive machinery, I was on foot heaving hay bales, pulling thistles, and walking row after row of beans. My dad interrupted my fog with "Okay, are you ready?" I slid over to the driver's side and he gave me a smile and said, "You can do this, I know you can," and waved goodbye. He didn't wait for a rebuttal or a response. I rolled up my window and proceeded to place this massive semi-tractor trailer truck in gear to start the journey. The journey was from our family acreage/farm to the new home Dave and I had recently purchased together when we were first married.

Will I make it alive? Could I make it alive? What am I doing?
I had no idea how to do it and I couldn't predict the ending.

This home was a fixer-upper; we knew it, but we loved the space, layout, and most of all the location. Most of all, it was ours, our first home together. Well, the inspection came back that the roof needed to be replaced, but what we didn't know until we had torn off the shingles was the sub-boards needed to be replaced as well. All the wood was rotted and a mess. We had to quickly switch gears to ordering and picking up wood and finding a way to dispose of all the rotten wood because the little dumpster for the shingles would not be able to hold the additional materials.

Dave asked me to call my dad to see if he could bring us one of his grain trucks to use to dispose of the rotten wood. My dad picked up the phone and instantly I knew he had a lot going on by the hurriedness in his voice. I quickly explained our situation and he said, "Come out and we will figure out what to do." I thought, *sure, I will drive out there and we will figure it out.*

Never did I ever imagine the "figure something out" would equate to me driving a grain truck for the very first time in my life. Never did I ever imagine driving a grain truck for the very first time in my life on a journey that included dirt roads and several small towns on multiple interstate systems and through my very own neighborhood.

With my mom following me in her vehicle, we started the journey. I took it slow on the dirt roads, and as I slid into the first small town, I quickly remembered how to drive a manual. For a moment I thought about my first car, a Mustang II, a manual vehicle, and it all came rushing back. Let's face it, small towns are filled with many stop signs and lights, lots of stops and starts, and now add in a big grain truck, an inexperienced driver, and well, who knows what was going to happen. My learning was that yellow lights mean go faster because there was no way to stop this thirty-ton moving truck.

We made it through the several smallish towns and found our way to the first interstate system. Sweat was dripping off of me, my hands tightly held onto the wheel. I thought, *I am staying in one lane and one lane only until I remember I have to navigate a difficult interstate exchange to get to my destination.* I knew the speed limit was sixty-five miles per hour and I was probably only going forty-five miles per hour because of how scared I was until I could make it to another straight away. I saw my exit coming up and I was beginning to relax, thinking, *I'm almost there!* I exited to the right, took an immediate left down a winding hill, and I felt a bit like a pro at that point.

I took the final left on Bedford Avenue to head up the hill to our home, and as I was coming roaring up the street, I found the big horn to the left of me and hit it twice, *Honkkkkk honnnnnnkkkkkk!* On top of the roof was my Dave and ten of his closest friends and coworkers staring with their mouths widely open. Remember, my dad was supposed to be driving! I had the biggest smile on my face and hit the brake. Dave yelled to me to back up in the driveway. *Oh great, my next challenge!* Yet again, there was someone who believed in me more than I believed in myself at that moment.

It took a small brave move to jump in the front seat of that truck knowing I had no idea how the story would end.

I am writing this book in the middle of a pandemic, a pandemic that was only supposed to last a few weeks and has now turned into almost a year. This pandemic that has created a tremendous amount of uncertainty in all aspects of our lives. We were unprepared for the pandemic even though we knew of pandemics, had experienced them before, and were able to predict what could happen. Still, we were not prepared.

We've known about racism, unresolved injustice and violence against the innocent by those with power. Still, the widespread demonstrations of 2020 were unexpected by many, and had unprecedented impact. How do we expect leaders to act in a chaotic, uncertain environment? Here is the thing, we can embrace the uncertainty of not knowing the result of the small brave moves we need to make. We just have to make one small brave move.

One day I was interviewing my client and friend, Lynda Shafer, about what was helping her be braver right now in the middle of the pandemic. She shared she was learning it's okay to be uncertain. "Just because you're uncertain doesn't mean you're not brave. So, embracing the uncertainty, I think is part of being braver. If you don't feel like you're doing what you were supposed to, what you've always done, what you were intended to do right now, don't doubt that important work remains. There's a lot of important work I need to get done in the world. So, be uncertain, but don't doubt."

EMBRACING UNCERTAINTY DEFINED

Embracing uncertainty involves being prepared to sit with a situation in all its uncertainty for as long as it takes for us to be sure we've seen it from all angles, until we know the response we have come up with is that which is the most compassionate and ethical possible under the circumstances and for all involved (including ourselves and others).

The only constant we will have in our lives is uncertainty.

Change will accompany us throughout our lives.

The ability to embrace uncertainty or even handle it is a principle of brave leaders.

BY EMBRACING UNCERTAINTY, YOU ACCEPT RISK

On December 5, 2007, nineteen-year-old Robert Hawkins walked into the luxury department store, Von Maur, during a psychotic break. An AK47 semi-automatic rifle and 692 rounds of armor piecing ammunition changed the lives of many who were there that day.

John McDonald, a sixty-five-year-old retiree, grabbed a chair—the chair in which he and his wife, Kathy, had been sitting on—and moved it behind her. For safety, he followed quickly as well. Just then, he heard the gunman approach about fifteen feet away, shooting at the employees behind the customer service counter. John stood up from his crouched hiding position to stand in front of his wife, who was still hiding behind the chair. Now face-to-face with the active shooter, John said, "Put the gun down. I can help you."

When John stood up and approached the active shooter, he accepted the risk and uncertainty of what would happen next. What John likely did not know was his interaction would cause the active shooter to turn his gun on himself, ending his life after he shot and killed John. Could John's confrontation with the active shooter have saved countless others lives? The active shooter still had plenty of ammunition. He could have gone on killing so many more. Dramatic acts like this one flow out of a practice of making brave choices in daily life, practicing small bravery.

My husband and the Special Weapons and Tactics (SWAT) team were some of the first responders that day. They had just finished doing security detail for President George W. Bush. President Bush attended a healthcare meeting at the

One World Community Health Center in Omaha, Nebraska that day. I remember Dave calling me to tell me in four seconds or less what was happening, and he said he would keep me posted.

I said "I love you" as I heard the click on the other end.

We had an understanding from years earlier that regardless of what he was dealing with, he would give me a heads-up and then text every few hours "ok" just to let me know he was safe. Why? On August 20, 1995, I was out to dinner with my family celebrating my little brother's birthday. When I got home, I had countless missed calls and voicemails on our voicemail machine. Before cell phones, we had these little recording machines to capture our messages. As I listened to the messages, it became clear that the wife of Dave's partner believed Dave and JP had been shot and possibly killed. I remember bursting into tears and calling Ginny back right away.

Dave had a pager at this time and was not responding to my pages. My heart sank. I lived in pure terror and fear for many hours and then finally received a call from Dave. He was only a few blocks away when Officer Jimmy Wilson was shot and killed. On Dave's mind wasn't *let me call my wife and let her know I am okay*, but rightfully so, *how do I help my brother in blue?* Dave and I were engaged, and I knew I never wanted to feel that way ever again. Every day when he leaves for work, I have to embrace the uncertainty he may never come home again with the roles he holds within the Omaha Police Department. Even after almost thirty years, I worry, even though I know how incredibly skilled he is at what he does.

Brave Leaders accept that life brings no guarantees, no matter how hopeful they are. They will always do their best to make the most of every situation.

In the book *The Possibility Principle*, Mel Schwartz discusses the need to embrace uncertainty: "Uncertainty is the correlative of change and possibility... But when we accept that all of life is uncertain... we can recover our human potential."[43]

Drs. Randall P. White and Sandra L. Shullman have identified a wide variety of leadership modes or ideals to fit newer paradigms because there is the need to be comfortable navigating ambiguous situations. One of the metrics indicative of this skill is the capacity to effectively process the uncertainty that often accompanies ambiguity. They were featured authors in the April 2010 issue of *CLO Magazine*. Writing on ambiguity leadership, White and Shullman advance the idea that an aptitude for ambiguity and the ability to be comfortable amidst uncertainty are traits that can be measured and developed. Also, they assert research suggests they are traits of high performers.[44]

---

43 Mel Schwartz, *The Possibility Principle: How Quantum Physics Can Improve the Way You Think, Live and Love* (Boulder: Sounds True, 2017).

44 Randal P. White, "Ambiguity Leadership: It's OK to Be Uncertain," *Chief Learning Officer*, March 28, 2010.

"What you know isn't as important as you think"

—NEIL DEGRASSE TYSON

Jeff Shannon, my business partner, recently shared the above quote with me and went on to say, "I think about…you could spend a lot of energy on knowing, when are things going back to normal? It's more important to say, it doesn't matter when it goes back to normal. How are you thinking about things right now? For me, its focus on adding value and coming up with new ways to add value. I'll give you an example. I was leading a virtual workshop on credibility with a sales team. Due to quarantining, the sales team can't get out there and see their clients and are having to do it virtually. One of the salespeople that were on the call said, *'Jeff, I'm not sure why initiative is something that's that important for us because I feel like we're all salespeople. We're driven people. We don't really need to talk about initiative. We get it.'*

I found that really interesting because her hang up was, *'I can't get in front of the client like I used to. I can't be live with them anymore. Therefore, I'm not sure what I can do.'* That, for me, is a really great example of not thinking about it correctly. She knows how to sell in one particular way. She's not focused on how she can think about this differently and actually take more initiative." Being a leader in this time means looking for the opportunities versus being reactive.

"Uncertainty is the only certainty there is."

—JOHN ALLEN PAULOS, MATHEMATICIAN

Based on interviews with numerous C-level executives around the world, Elizabeth Mellon—executive director of Duke Corporate Education—said mindset, more than personality and behavior, forms an observable pattern among some of the most successful leaders and that a fearless approach to uncertainty is required.[45]

---

45   Ibid.

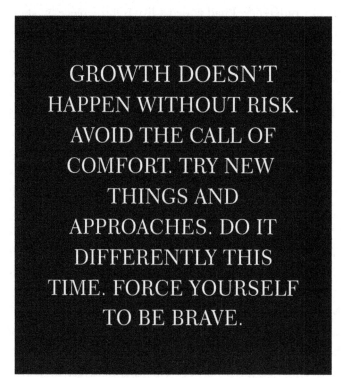

GROWTH DOESN'T HAPPEN WITHOUT RISK. AVOID THE CALL OF COMFORT. TRY NEW THINGS AND APPROACHES. DO IT DIFFERENTLY THIS TIME. FORCE YOURSELF TO BE BRAVE.

Getting comfortable being uncomfortable is one of our values at Bravium HD.

We do this because you can easily fall into the trap of doing the same thing over and over and then growth slows down. Every time we launch an offsite, workshop, program, or speaking gig, we try something new—something that will either be successful or will fail, and we never know at the start. When it works better than you even imagined and the crowd goes wild, it is so rewarding!

I was preparing for an upcoming keynote labeled "How Spicy Do You Want It?" at a Society for Human Resources Management Conference. I had added a live improv piece on stage and was nervous. What if it flops? What if the volunteers who chose to come up are not into it? I had practiced it over and over, yet there was so much I could not control about the variables. I wasn't sure if I could pull it off because it was risky. The volunteers raised their hands and jumped up on stage as I was quickly giving instructions for the various pieces. We were off and running. The audience was going wild, laughing, and clapping as if the volunteers were improv pros. It was amazing! I took a deep breath after and was so thankful it worked. It doesn't always work, though.

Another time I was doing a keynote on being a braver leader. I decided to take a risk and do live coaching. I asked a volunteer to take the stage with me, and we sat in two chairs. My goal was to explore and coach them for about ten minutes in front of a live audience to demonstrate the power of being there for each other. A few minutes into the coaching it became clear the volunteer had other motives. They were not interested in exploring how they could be a braver leader. The motive was that they wanted to find a new job and the room was filled with human resources executives and leaders. My heart sank. I did my best in those ten minutes, but it failed; I failed. Getting comfortable being uncomfortable means we are taking risks, and those risks may not play out the way we intended. We learn and we move on.

We have to be comfortable stepping out of our comfort zone. We need to make a decision and decide to decide. Not every decision we make will be right. The important thing is to be brave enough to move forward, even in a small way. When we decide to move forward, we will learn the consequences of our decisions. When we know the consequences, we can adapt, change directions as needed, and make the next decision. Staying in our comfort zone ensures we go nowhere.

Seth Godin, entrepreneur and best-selling author, shares that before we make a decision, we wonder about our dreams, stories, and needs. We wonder to ourselves the unspoken questions:

Is this good for me right now?

Will this make me feel dumb?

Does it raise my status?

Will this help me be a part of a group I care about?

Would my mom be proud of me?

Will I get blamed?

Is there a shortcut?

Is it safe?

Is it thrilling?[46]

---

46 Seth Godin, "The Unspoken Questions," *Seth's Blog,* November 5, 2020.

These questions Godin poses help us decide whether to embrace the uncertainty. Uncertainty is a certain thing. All of life has at least a bit of uncertainty attached to it, and sometimes a lot of uncertainty, that may take a very long time to resolve. You cannot know how everything is going to unfold. Even things you feel so sure of and dependent upon can change.

People get caught up in the idea of things lasting "forever." But they frequently don't. Being aware of the possibility that things can change can help you cope if things happen that you didn't expect. It's not that you need to live in fear of things changing and ending but being prepared for the possibility can help you be more resilient and flexible when things do happen.[47]

BRAVERSHIP HABITS TO EMBRACE UNCERTAINTY
1. **Zero in on what you can control.**

Even while you're going through change and uncertainty, there are many pieces of your life you can count on to stay stable and reliable. Identify the aspects you can control and use them as a framework around which to build the rest of your life.

Establish a daily routine that helps you move through your day. The habitual and familiar will help you feel more grounded in your life even when things feel up in the air.

---

47 Christine Carter, "Seven Ways to Cope with Uncertainty," *Greater Good Science Center at Berkley*, July 27, 2020.

The habitual and routine provide a safety net, something to help you feel your life is not in free fall.

When the pandemic hit and all of a sudden our entire business came to a screeching halt, we established 8:00 a.m. calls for thirty minutes every day to create our plan for the day. Looking back, those calls saved me. I required myself to get up and get ready for the day before the call. The call motivated me to move past the uncertainty and create new value for our clients, for our business.

In addition to a daily routine, create moments that help you enjoy your life as it is. No sense in sitting around terrified about the future. That will sort itself out. Stay positive and hopeful that somehow things will work out, even if you have no idea how that will happen.

2. **Engage in things that are goal oriented.**
Not goal directed for the future, but goal oriented for the day or week. Projects or hobbies that can give you a sense of accomplishment and allow you to have an outcome of certainty can be soothing. I have to remind myself to set small goals in the personal project or hobby area, otherwise work overshadows them.

We could not dine out much during the pandemic and I had more time on my hands because I wasn't commuting to and from work. I decided I wanted to cook more elaborate and delicious meals. Taking sixty to ninety minutes at the end of a workday to listen to music and create extraordinary food dishes became so therapeutic for me. It allowed me to create and relax at the same time and it forced me to move away from my home office and transition into being home.

3. Embrace "the suck."

If the situation is bad, deal with it. Don't just deal with it, open your arms and welcome it. Just when you think things couldn't get any worse, it is here. "The suck" is here to make you tougher. If you are embracing "the suck" by yourself, laugh at how ridiculous the situation is. You are building your mental and physical toughness points. Embracing "the suck" in a group is a powerful bonding experience.

We were going through "the suck" when my daughter, who is a collegiate track and field athlete, was at indoor nationals in Birmingham, Alabama. She was training two days before nationals was to start when they were told to go home. Indoor Track and Field Nationals was cancelled due to COVID. As she came home and we were quarantining for what we thought was a month or so, we began to come up with a word of the day to shake our heads at the day before and be proactively prepared for "the suck" of what the new day was going to bring. Sharing it with her was powerful. We moved through it, we laughed, we cried, and we learned.

4. Find meaning in the chaos.

Social psychologists define meaning, as it applies to our lives, as "an intellectual and emotional assessment of the degree to which we feel our lives have purpose, value, and impact."[48] We humans are best motivated by our significance to other people. We'll work harder and longer and better and feel happier about the work we are doing when we know someone else is benefiting from our efforts. Sometimes we know our clients need us, but we aren't quite sure what they need. We listen a lot and work to show up in ways to add purpose, value, and impact. Ask yourself, "What value can I add today?"

5. Utilize stress reduction techniques preemptively. When we are dealing with uncertainty, we have stress in our bodies, even if it's not at the forefront of our thoughts in this exact moment. Over time, that body stress affects blood pressure, blood sugar, muscle tension, cholesterol level, breathing rate, and every organ in your body.[49] Incorporate stress reduction techniques into your day, ideally meditation, even if for just five to ten minutes daily. Breathing exercises can be a powerful way to center our body and refocus. Music can also be another powerful tool to shift our thinking. Finding your center will help you feel better prepared to tackle whatever comes your way.

THE CLIMB

I haven't been able to climb a mountain for a very long time. Why? I have suffered from severe stage four osteoarthritis arthritis in both knees. Most days it was painful to just do the basics like walking. Early in 2020, I received a total knee

---

48 Christine Carter, "Seven Ways to Cope with Uncertainty," *Greater Good*, July 27, 2020

49 "Stress Effects on the Body," American Psychological Association (American Psychological Association), accessed March 5, 2021.

replacement on my left knee, a surgery not for the weak of heart. Only around six months later, I feel like a new person—well 50 percent newer.

Dave, Nic, and I recently went on a road trip during COVID just to get out of town. One of the stops recommended was Toadstool Geological Park in western Nebraska. I stood there at the bottom of this intimidating terrain telling myself there was no way I could climb it with only one good knee. Dave and Nic had gone the other way, the long way around, to climb to the top so I was alone. I wanted to surprise them and meet them toward the top. The terrain was tricky and there was one narrowing point where, with one wrong move, I would be tumbling all the way down.

Silly, I know. We tell ourselves stories and allow uncertainty and fear in. I knew the bravest thing I needed to do right then was to start the climb.

I might fail.

I might fall.

I might only make it part of the way with one good knee.

Nothing was certain.

✓ I just needed to try.
✓ I reminded myself failure is a part of the journey and to keep climbing.
✓ We don't have to do it alone. This photo was taken by Dave and Nic, who helped me make this happen.

Brave leaders know uncertainty offers chances to create something new.

11.

HOPE DRIVEN

"We can't change what life hands us, but each of our lives is a gift. Find every moment you can to breathe hope into everything you do."

—BETZ, MY MOM

In April 2015, I was getting ready to announce a new and innovative leadership program when a chance encounter became a fulfillment of a promise I thought might have slipped away. The past five months had been extremely tough grieving the loss of my mom and turning back "on" a business I had put on hold to care for her during her final months. My heart ached for her every day, and I was still trying to figure out how to live without her.

On November 15, 2012, our family was blindsided by my mom's diagnosis of late stage IV lung cancer that had metastasized to her bones. She was only given two months to live. Hearing those words, I felt the breath escape my lungs. All of life flashed through my mind. I was devastated. Cancer had already shaken our family to the core in 1999 when my father, Rich Giese, passed away after a six-month battle with esophageal cancer. The speed at which his life ended was jarring and difficult to comprehend. We fought hard but were ill-equipped for the journey. We had no idea it could happen so fast.

My mom, Betz, was determined to fight, and we were determined to surround her with love and advocacy every step of the way. My mom was always a light even in the darkest of situations. She lifted everyone she knew with her spirit and sense of humor. During her fight, purple became her signature color and even amidst excruciating pain, her amazing smile and words of wisdom and encouragement were never far from her lips. "Brave" by Sara Bareilles was her theme song, and her personal bravery was inspirational and infectious to everyone she encountered.

The prognosis of two months turned into nearly two years and included many amazing memories as a family allowing us all to live more intentionally. We did so many things together including a family vacation to the Florida beaches, and it was the first time she was able to stand on a beach surrounded by all of her grandchildren. We were so blessed to have these moments with her.

In October 2014, during one of our last conversations, she told me her life would soon be ending. As we held hands and I cried, she told me she would always be with me. Choking back the sobs, I asked her, "How will I know?" She simply said, "Look for butterflies, purple butterflies." My mom lost her battle with cancer on Oct 22, 2014, just two weeks shy of the goal she set for herself. She left behind instructions to our family to live life to the fullest.

Fast forward to April 2015. I sat at the Women's Leadership Conference waiting to announce the new program we had developed in front of 2,500 women business leaders. It was a pivotal moment for my business, a business that thrived in part because of who my mom challenged me to be. At the conference, I was sitting next to my friend Joey Patterson. She looked at me as she was reading a new twitter notification. She said, "Oh my gosh Nicole, there is a purple butterfly, it is a scavenger hunt." Right here, right now, a purple butterfly?

A keynote speaker, Erik Wahl, who had just finished his revolutionary keynote using speed-painting and graffiti to share his leadership message, began to leave these clues at the conference via Twitter. Joey and I stared at each other for a few seconds and, with trembling hands, started to follow the clues on Twitter.

We often hear, "Hope is not a plan," or, "Hope is not a strategy," let alone a strategy for action. Hope is the fundamental belief that change is possible and the expectation that it is our actions, fueled by a positive vision of the future that drive successful outcomes. The concept of *Hope Theory*, the science of hopefulness, was pioneered by the late Dr. C.R. Snyder, a professor of psychology at the University of Kansas at Lawrence. Dr. Snyder defined hope as based on both *"willpower"* and *"way-power,"* where one is able not only to create multiple pathways to realizing a vision, but also to sustain the mental energy and perseverance to travel those pathways effectively.[50]

With the uncertainty caused by the COVID-19 outbreak, it is critical leaders instill their workforce with a hope-driven view of the future as well as a concrete action plan to adapt and innovate for a changed world. Leaders all respond differently to crisis. Some of us switch into "action" mode and become more transactional in how we interact with others. Some of us go quiet and withdraw. Times of crisis can provide some of the most important opportunities to deepen trust and commitment with our teams in ways that not only ensure greater well-being for employees, but also positions the department/organization to recover when the crisis is over.

---

50   C.R. Snyder, *Handbook of Hope Theory, Measures and Applications* (San Diego: Academic Press; 2000), 3–21.

Feelings, fears, and frustrations can lead us down a path of hopelessness.

Hope is a positive expectation of a better future.

WHAT IS HOPE?

Hope is associated with many positive outcomes, including greater happiness, better academic achievement, and even lowered risk of death. It's a necessary ingredient for getting through tough times, of course, but also for meeting everyday goals. Everyone benefits from having hope—and psychologists' research suggests almost anyone can be taught to be more hopeful. "Hope doesn't relate to IQ or to income," says psychologist Shane Lopez, PhD, a senior scientist at Gallup and author of the 2013 book *Making Hope Happen*. "Hope is an equal opportunity resource."[51]

What precisely is hope? Most psychologists who study the feeling favor the definition developed by hope research pioneer, the late Charles R. Snyder, PhD. His model of hope has three components: goals, agency, and pathways. "Put simply, agency is our ability to shape our lives—the belief we can make things happen, and the motivation to reach a desired outcome. The pathways are how we get there—the routes and plans that allow us to achieve the goal, whether that's

---

51 Shane J. Lopez, *Making Hope Happen: Create the Future You Want for Yourself and Others* (New York: Atria Paperback; 2013), 96.

adopting a child, finding a better job, surviving a hurricane, or just losing a few pounds."[52]

Hope is more than just a state of mind; it is an action-oriented strength. In the absence of this inner resource, how can we find the motivation to pursue our goals and the resilience to pick ourselves up when things go wrong? Many people persevere with the idea that hope is an either/or proposition, believing that to have hope, all despair must be extinguished. While it is true that hope comes and goes, and there are times when we feel like all hope is diminished, a light at the end of the tunnel is a representation of the hope that everyone can hold tight and use to persevere.

GROWING OUR HOPE

In my interview with Leia Baez, an award-winning journalist, motivational speaker, and success coach, she shared how storytelling can help us grow hope—both ours and others. Back in 2015, Leia went through a terrible divorce and custody battle for her daughter. She moved back in with her parents to get back on her feet. She was chosen to give her commencement speech for her MBA and shared her story.

She had the opportunity to share her story of divorce, custody, and going back to school as a single parent. Immediately following her speech, someone came up and said to Leia, "your story gives me hope, I am going to push through." Just

---

52 C.R. Snyder, *Handbook of Hope Theory, Measures and Applications* (San Diego: Academic Press, 2000), 3–21.

then Leia knew she had to continue to share her story of courage and bravery to give hope to others.

SHARING HOPE

A dear friend of mine, Teresa Kopietz, had a dream after her mom, Joan Garro, passed away. In the dream, a message was clear: create a night of inspiration and happiness to share with others. In life, it is easy to dwell on the negative things and forget about all the blessings that surround us. Each of us will face tough challenges in our lives. Teresa struggled to know what to do with this message. She gathered with a few friends and "A Night of Hope" was born to share stories of survivors and challenges they faced through their personal journeys.

She intended for it to be a one-time event, and it celebrated its sixth year in 2020! The act of creating an evening for others to restore their hope and find possibilities in so many tough challenges and scenarios is a great example of sharing hope. I had the opportunity to take the stage in 2019 and share how we found hope after losing both my mother and father to cancer. The speakers during those events provide a container to share powerful stories, ultimately sharing hope with others.

Brave Leaders consistently imagine a better world than the one they currently live in. They turn their dreams into concrete goals built upon their purpose and ethos.

Hope starts with a belief that change is possible and then an expectation that what you do as an individual is what makes the difference. You determine the outcome. It's not determined by your leader or your spouse or the world at large. It's up to you.

When you put those together with a future vision that is so intense and so inspiring, then you have to be able to articulate that to others. You have to find your own reasons to have hope and then lead yourself using that hope. Find ways to share your hope with others to inspire and inform rather than demand and give orders.

When people feel lost, uncertain, and troubled in their careers and lives, sometimes all they want is a dose of hope. Much like happiness, hope is an emotion that comes and goes. It requires the individual to make intentional choices to sustain its positive impact. As such, the workplace culture, the people you associate yourself with, and your general state of mind are just a few things that influence your degree of happiness and hope. Hopeful individuals possess positive thinking that is reflective of a realistic sense of optimism as well as the belief they can produce routes to desired goals, according to Daniel Goleman in *Emotional Intelligence*.[53]

Many just want to hear a leader tell them that everything is going to be fine. They want a sense of security, a feeling that their worries and sorrows will soon be gone. As we all know about life, you are either solving a problem, coming out of a problem, or heading into a new problem. Hope alleviates the tension points throughout life's journey.

Brave Leaders always maintain a positive outlook on life no matter how grim or dire the situation. This is of course only possible because they are highly attuned to their negative thoughts. The moment negative thoughts take over, they immediately switch gears and reframe their experience.

Hopeful people seek support from others, problem-solve, or tell themselves positive statements to keep them motivated. Sometimes they even modify their goals. Either way, *they are able to pick themselves up and find other ways to tackle their*

---

53 D. Goleman, *Emotional Intelligence: Why It Can Matter More Than IQ* (New York: Bloomsbury Publishing PLC, 1996), 252.

challenges and keep moving ahead. Research also shows us that people who are hopeful are more satisfied with life, have higher academic achievement and are better able to manage physical and mental health concerns.

The beauty of hope is we can teach it to others, model it for our teams, and work on building our own hope each day.

How many times have you encountered an obstacle on the way to a goal? This is pretty much an hourly occurrence for most humans. We spill coffee in the morning, we're running late to drop off the kids, we feel tired after a bad night of sleep, or we're experiencing conflict with someone.

Obstacles are prominent in everyone's lives, and being hopeful gives us a road map for how to navigate them and move toward our goals.

Below are some exercises to develop your hopeful road map:

1. Spend some time each day thinking about your goals. Try to identify the small wins (short-term goals) you want to get done that day, as well as the larger goals you would like to work toward over the next days and weeks. The small wins create momentum.
2. Talk with your circle about your goals, as well as theirs. Describe the obstacles coming up for you and brainstorm ways to support one another as you navigate the challenges.
3. Obstacles will always interfere with our plans. However, we must embrace the idea that what stands in the way becomes the way. We will endure, adapt, and overcome.

Pause and remind yourself everyone faces obstacles toward the goals they want to achieve.

4. Consider how you want to model hope for others. How do you want them to see you handling obstacles? Don't be afraid to say your hopeful thoughts out loud (for example, "Okay, we can't find the right building, but we are going to ask for help and we'll be able to find it. We'll figure this out.").

5. Periodically review your goals and see which ones need to be revised. Think carefully about which goals stretch you in positive ways, and which might not be realistic. Remember that part of the joy of hope is you can adapt and create new goals if you need to!

"Hope is a good thing, maybe the best of things, and no good thing ever dies. I will be hoping this letter finds you and finds you well."

—*SHAWSHANK REDEMPTION*[54]

NURTURING HOPE

Hope is a powerful force that brings people together. It instills a sense of unity, collective pride, and strengthens optimism when people work together as one. This is why team building is so powerful. By leveraging one another's

---

54 Frank Darbout, The Shawshank Redemption, United States: Columbia Pictures; 1994.

unique strengths and capabilities, we become more hopeful and can accomplish much more.

Start each day with a moment of intention and gratitude:

- What are the three things you are most grateful for?
- What intentions do you want to set out for the day?

End each day with:

- A peak to celebrate from today.
- A valley to reflect on from today.
- A blessing you didn't expect.

In a recent interview with Daniel Pink, he shared that we don't always have a sense of progress. Because of this, he has created a ritual where he ends each day memorializing progress. He says:

"Take a moment, this ritual is important. Ask yourself, what did I get done today? You get more done than you thought."

THE PURPLE BUTTERFLY LANDS

Back to the scavenger hunt. We quickly realized where it was, and I took off running. This beautiful purple butterfly was face down resting in the hands of a sculpted mime statue in front of the downtown convention center in Omaha, Nebraska, about two hundred meters from where I was. My hands were trembling as I lifted the purple butterfly from the statue's hands. I was light-headed and weak as I began to realize what this meant.

I was the first person to find it. Out of 2,800 leaders who were following the scavenger hunt, it was me. My mom said to look for her in butterflies—purple butterflies—and six months later I found her, a beautiful purple butterfly.

As I walked back into the Women's Leadership Conference, Sara Bareilles' song "Brave" was being belted out by a singer on the main stage. I felt like I might faint as I was flooded with my mom's presence. I was clutching a beautiful purple butterfly in my trembling hands. My heart was bursting, yet such a wave of peace settled over me. I knew she was with me.

Being hope driven enabled me to see the butterfly, to be present, and to connect with my mom.

Brave Leaders find every moment to breathe hope into everything they do.

PART III

ONE SMALL BRAVE MOVE AT A TIME

12.

BUILDING A CULTURE
OF BRAVERSHIP

———

"While successful culture can look and feel like
magic, the truth is that it's not. Culture is a set of
living relationships working toward a shared goal.
It's not something you are. It's something you do."

—DANIEL COYLE, *THE CULTURE CODE: THE*
SECRETS OF HIGHLY SUCCESSFUL GROUPS

BUILD THE CULTURE FROM SCRATCH

When we built our company Bravium HD, almost nine years ago, we wanted to be intentional about the culture we were creating. Jeff and I had both worked in departments and organizations where culture wasn't always the top focus or even a priority. For us that would be different. We didn't wait for the business to be built; we started with the culture we both wanted and what it would take to make it happen. Here is where we started:

LOOK IN THE MIRROR

An acute and accurate awareness of yourself, starting with your weak spots or triggers, can inform your culture-building path. Do you try to control others when you're stressed? Do you avoid difficult conversations? Imagine your worst qualities amplified in a group of people because you inadvertently normalize behaviors that have tripped you up. Your leadership needs to be the picture of the ideal culture.

BUILD IT AROUND TRUST + RESPECT

There are many aspects to a strong organizational culture and if you build it around "trust" and "respect" for each other as individuals, it becomes much easier to meet the challenges of company growth and crisis situations that require trust and cohesiveness to see them through. This creates safety, allowing for open dialogue, honest feedback, and creativity.

BE THE CULTURE, MODEL THE WAY

As a leader, you don't work in a culture, you are the culture. As the organization is growing, you are under constant observation. So, watch what you are saying, what you are doing, and how you are doing it. Follow the principle of "show them, don't tell them." Don't tell your team you value their health, give them flexible working hours. Don't say you have a feedback culture, have the tough conversations, talk straight. Walk the talk. Being a role model of the culture, you want to see in your organization is the most powerful tool you have.

CREATE A CULTURE PLAYBOOK

Culture playbooks set the tone, capture the tone, and continue the tone of what right looks like inside of your company walls. Create your culture statement based on what you think, believe, do, say, see, and hear around your vision, mission, and value statements. Capturing it in writing, on videos, and in pictures from every team member joining along the way keeps the culture guardrails on.

BE CLEAR ABOUT YOUR "WHY"

Leaders will be measured on one thing alone: culture. As leaders, we can move so quickly to the "doing," we rarely stop in the early days to make sure everyone is clear on the "why." Carve out time each week to share with the team "why" decisions were made, systems were created, what's coming up next, and why it matters. Tell your story often. Our why?

> Inspire functional experts to transform
> into strategic leaders.

HERE IS HOW IT PLAYS OUT IN EVERYTHING WE DO:

Transformation is that strange tickle that shows up just before you summon the courage to take the field, go on stage, or ride the roller coaster with the two-hundred-foot drop. When did you last have that sensation? When did you last have that sensation at work?

If you're like most people, it's been a while—or never. Few of us have these feelings at work because we tend to avoid decisions or actions that require bravery. We naturally prefer the comfort of the status quo and the safety of the crowd. We play small just like everybody else. As a result, we seldom take opportunities to transform ourselves, our teammates, or our organization.

At Bravium, we approach "butterflies" a little differently. We celebrate this magical feeling and believe it's a sign we're about to do something remarkable. We embrace these moments of bravery as the truest way of achieving our highest potential.

With this spirit in mind, we design experiences and training programs that help individuals and teams bravely transform into more strategic, innovative, and effective leaders.

CREATE YOUR VALUES

Starting your own business means you have the opportunity to do things your way. This is your chance to create a thriving company culture that aligns with your leadership style, not someone else's. Your vibe will attract the right people who value the work you do and the impactful culture you're building. Your vibe comes out in your culture and is grounded on values.

In setting a new culture, I would talk to clients and employees on what we have stood for in the past, what has made us unique, and what has led to predictable behaviors that lead to results. This helps us understand our actual values and helps us create them to build the future.

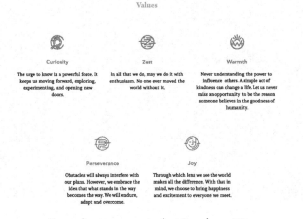

Values

Curiosity

The urge to know is a powerful force. It keeps us moving forward, exploring, experimenting, and opening new doors.

Zest

In all that we do, may we do it with enthusiasm. No one ever moved the world without it.

Warmth

Never understanding the power to influence others. A simple act of kindness can change a life. Let us never miss an opportunity to be the reason someone believes in the goodness of humanity.

Perseverance

Obstacles will always interfere with our plans. However, we embrace the idea that what stands in the way becomes the way. We will endure, adapt and overcome.

Joy

Through which lens we see the world makes all the difference. With that in mind, we choose to bring happiness and excitement to everyone we meet.

Our values we created at Bravium, HD.

BUILD YOUR OPERATING PRINCIPLES IN AN UNORTHODOX WAY

Jeff and I looked at all the activities and behaviors we didn't want to see in Bravium HD and turned them into operating principles for our team to follow. For example, we didn't want our team to feel as if we had to say yes to every client all the time. So, we built "hold the line" into our operating principles, and it reminds us and gives us permission to bless and release any person or project that is not in alignment with how we operate. It is clear.

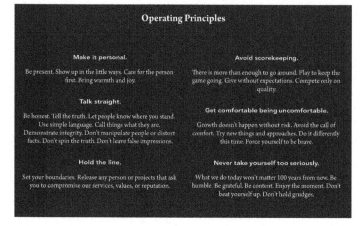

Our Operating Principles we created at Bravium HD.

CULTIVATE CONNECTION WITH YOUR TEAM

Regardless of the size of your team, you can develop a strong culture within your business by building intentional relationships with them. Avoid the call of "busyness" and invest time to connect. Ask yourself how you can create deeper connections with those on your team. What common values do you share and how can you work together toward a common mission you are all passionate about?

TALK ABOUT EXPECTATIONS OVER AND OVER

Consciously articulate expectations repeatedly in all you do. Expectations drive clarity, inspire, and challenge people to stretch themselves. Being clear on expectations creates alignment among you and the team.

FIXING A BROKEN CULTURE TO BUILD THE RIGHT CULTURE

People's confidences were down. They didn't trust the last president, and rightfully so. He never showed up on time for meetings, he didn't trust them to do their jobs, and he micromanaged their every move.

Our new president at Conagra Frozen Foods, Dean Hollis, oversaw this transformation. He started with trust. Past leadership had destroyed trust and rebuilding was needed for us to deliver strong results. He shared with us the Chinese symbol for trust, 相信, and told us it means a leader who stands behind his words and actions. He knew he had to earn this for us to follow him. We needed to know he had our backs. Dean was clear with us. He wanted us to know that things will be hard, and we will be okay. The expectations were clear. We worked hard to keep alignment, we were empowered and held accountable for what and how we would deliver. Dean exemplified this.

In a recent interview with Dean talking about how he approached it, he shared, "Trust is reciprocal. It is complete trust and confidence, in someone or something. So, if you think about all the uncertainty that's going on and what people are really looking for, is it going to be okay? Do I trust that we are going to be okay? Are we going to make it? Whether it's personally or health wise, safety wise or business wise. That's where leaders really have to step in. Our role, above everything else, is to demonstrate our complete confidence and trust, in these times of uncertainty. So, my word is faith and within that confidence and trust."

I was in the right role, right place, and right time when Dean began casting a clear and compelling vision for what needed to be done and supporting each of us to understand how we could help. Dean embraced human resources as a partner in strategy and change, which was new and refreshing. We had to change the culture from one of *blaming and finger pointing at other function or departments, corporate, or each other as individuals,* to a culture of *working and winning together.*

As you can imagine, not all leaders were on board in the beginning. We had to listen for and identify where organizationally the new culture was not being implemented and take action to correct across the enterprise. Embedding this culture change lower than the VP level was a challenge due to time pressures and work volumes. Jeff Branstetter, the vice president of human resources, shared in an interview, "My bravery came in to challenge my peers to adopt the practices we agreed upon...sometimes easy, sometimes a real battle. We had to change leaders out to make the changes...while still achieving results."

The transformation occurred over three years and was focused on empowering, enabling, and enlightening. Each year, Dean shared a clear vision for where we needed to go and how we would get there at our annual company meetings.

- Year 1: Follow the Flag up the hill in battle, where we had to rally as a team and seize today (Carpe Diem) and tomorrow (Carpe Manana), as the executive team did a skit from *Star Trek,* pretending the ship was damaged and shaking, and we were under attack. The message was clear, we needed to rally together and follow the flag up the hill in the heat of the battle.

- Year 2: FASTER: Focused, Aligned, Simplify, Talk, Execute = Results as Dean entered our meeting in a go-kart, driving around Omaha to our site and onto the stage. The message was we were making strong progress, but we had to move faster.
- Year 3: Raise the Bar, get out of our comfort zone, and push ourselves to new heights. Dean announced our year three theme and mantra by entering our company-wide meeting sky diving. In year three, we were rocking and rolling, and the message was to grow the business and ourselves professionally.

Dean focused on being clear on vision and expectations and then inspiring us all to join him in what needed to be done. He was masterful at bringing others along with him. Each year the messages and the mantras showed up in everything Dean did from his daily moves, every meeting, and to our quarterly town halls. The clarity drove strong performance and results in the frozen foods business.

SET FIRE TO THIS CULTURE AND WALK AWAY

I received a call one evening from the raging Diet Coke leader you heard about in the Relentless Curiosity chapter.

She was the head of product development, and I was a director of human resources at the time. She was my internal client, and I was her strategic business partner. We had been working through some promotions together, and she had outlined who she wanted promoted and how much she wanted to give to them. She was basically handing me the piece of paper to process. She promoted four people not because of performance, but because they were her favorites, at the moment, and gave them huge increases without consideration for their compensation ranges or the market data.

I asked a few questions to help her think through the moves she wanted to make. Then moved to sharing the implications and impact on her broader leadership team, two of the leaders would be red circled. Being "red circled" meant you were at the top of your salary range, being paid above market, and would no longer receive merit increases.

We ended the meeting aligning on that she would think about it and we would discuss it further in the morning. My husband and I went out to dinner that evening, sans children, to a favorite restaurant downtown near our Conagra Foods campus. I had missed a call during dinner from the same leader I had met with earlier and noticed a voicemail. As we were walking back to our car, I played the voicemail so I could take care of what needed to be taken care of on our drive home.

The first words left were: Nicole, I have thought about our conversation, and if I wanted your fucking advice, I would have asked for it. Process the fucking promotions. Got it? *Loud bang* and the voicemail ended. My heart fell, thinking what on earth did I do to deserve this? Then it turned to nausea, the kind you feel when you may have been too brave and are now regretting it. Then I moved to pure anger, who the hell does she think she is? Thinking she can leave a voicemail like this? I didn't do anything wrong.

The next day, I walked in early to work as usual around 7:00 a.m., and before 7:30 a.m. I had three other executive leaders on her team stop into my office. Each one saying they had heard the message she had left for me the night before. By the time the third person had stopped into my office, I realized three things:

1. She had made an example of me, leaving her executive office door open so everyone could hear of my mistake and learn from it.
2. Each one of them had experienced something similar.
3. This leadership team had formed a support group, ready to swoop in and help each other through.

I took a deep breath and thought to myself, *now what?*

I knew I couldn't live in that toxic culture long-term. Now it was about choices, and I had to make a choice.

- Do nothing. See what happens. Move past it.
- Address the conflict directly and meet with her to discuss the voicemail.
- Elevate the issue. Elevate awareness to the pattern of behavior.

You have to choose what's best for you. Choice makes us vulnerable, so it makes us brave. I knew I had to make more than one choice. I had to make a series of small brave moves to address the much larger issue. My first small brave move was to elevate and go straight to the chief human resources officer (CHRO), two levels above me, and also a peer of the Diet Coke tyrant.

TAKE RESPONSIBILITY

True intentional leaders do not shy away from accepting responsibility when something goes wrong. Because intentional leaders think each decision over carefully, they will always be confident in the decision that was made, even if it doesn't have the best results. These leaders are ready to admit their faults and learn from their mistakes. But, as an intentional leader, it is up to you to move the entire team forward after a mistake. The team's attention must shift to focus on what needs to be done next and how to bounce back from the problem.

The culture at Conagra Foods at this time was one of command and control, bark and demand, no thinking, do as I tell you, "on call" day or night because the leaders could not organize their own thoughts, so we had to drop anything and everything whenever.

It was like being a short order cook at Waffle House.

We learn just as much from the bad leaders as we do the good ones.

A CULTURE OF APPRECIATION AND THANKS: FUELING OUR TEAM'S JOURNEY

One day, a friend of my daughter stopped by to give me a thank-you card as she was heading out for college. In that moment, I was thinking to myself, *what a thoughtful thing to do!* I opened the card not expecting to read the following:

I can't tell you what it's meant to me

to always feel so loved

and welcome in your home.

Some of my best memories from
senior year were at your house,

surrounded by love and laughter.

You've been such a fantastic role model,
and I truly look up to you.

Tears immediately rolled down my cheek. Why? Because I had only known this beautiful girl for a short time. I thought back to all these moments when we would open up our home to the girls, prepare appetizers, snacks, and lemonade as they got ready for a school event, game, or dance. What do I remember most? Chaos and laughter as the girls bustled to get prepared. This thank-you struck me. Why? (1) I never expected such a small act to have a significant impact. (2) The simple act of her taking the time to write a thank-you, a heartfelt thank-you made my heart sing!

We were closing a nine-month leadership program with an exercise to fuel the participants' leadership journey. The power of the activity is sharing a wish or appreciation on a small piece of paper for each participant and once read aloud it goes into a beautiful bowl. The bowl filled with these wishes and appreciations is what the leader carries forward with them on their journey. Imagine yourself having one of those days when nothing seems to be going right, maybe a project was canceled, you lost a star employee, or you were asked to take a role or project you aren't excited about.

Now, think about the days when something significant happens to you, you landed a big contract, your first article was published, or your new product landed on the shelves, maybe even a promotion or your dream job. Looking into that bowl at those who supported you along the way make the journey even more rewarding, right? When I started my company in 2012, I remember feeling how lonely it was. I no longer had a boss giving me words of appreciation or encouragement, my peer group sat within various companies, and some even became competitors.

As I began to work with clients, I would receive an email or note saying how much of an impact I had made on them. Wow, I thought! This is good stuff, stuff I need to take alongside me on my journey to remind me of the important work we are doing. Yes! I have a bowl I put emails of appreciation, notecards, cards, and even social media messages in. I look back into it from time to time. It reminds me of three things:

1. I am doing important work, and people appreciate it!
2. I am surrounded by people who will tell me when I am doing something well *and* also tell me when I need to get my act together.
3. Never, ever forget to show my appreciation and thanks. No matter how busy I get, send the thank-you, make the phone call, send the card.

One of the most unique graduation gifts my daughter, Moe, received was from my friend, Julie Schnepel. She gave her a pack of thank-you cards, stamps, and a pen. The note-card read:

> *You're going to have tough days and think what the hell have I gotten myself into.*
>
> *On those days I want you to think about a person who made a difference in your life. Now, I want you to write a thank-you note and let them know how they made a difference.*
>
> *And remember, they have days just like today too.*

Think about that for a minute. What a lesson!

I was coaching a leader from a Fortune 10 company who had just received feedback she rarely showed appreciation or thanks to her teams. This leader found the input devastating. She genuinely cared for her team, and she thought they knew that. There is a difference between caring and showing appreciation or thanks. She decided to create a new weekly habit. The new habit included her asking herself the following two questions at the end of the day:

> Who am I most grateful for today?
>
> Have I let them know?

WARNING! DON'T TRY THIS AT HOME! TRY IT AT WORK AND HOME!

For your next team meeting, bring a fun notecard for each person. Have the team divide into pairs. Share the following instructions: you have five minutes to find three strengths of the person you are paired up with. Use everyone or as many as you can from the team to gather this information quickly. At the end of the five minutes, return to your pairs and share what the team appreciates about your partner with them!

The hunt to find three strengths can be so much fun! Being the recipient of the card is even better!

What gets recognized gets repeated. If we take time to understand those strengths or appreciations, they will get repeated. As a leader, it's important to be intentional about giving thanks and appreciation.

What can you do this week to build or enhance your habits to include thanks for appreciation?

13.

HOW TO BECOME A BRAVER LEADER

"It takes courage to grow up and become who you really are."

—E.E. CUMMINGS

In 2019, we launched a session for a leadership development program. The program was designed to groom a group of executives for their next role. This level of leadership is challenging because they are supposed to be experts in so many things, but the reality is they are learning and growing at a rapid rate.

Knowing everything is impossible.

The fun part was everyone was so eager to learn!

GIVE YOURSELF PERMISSION

When you're in a group that is new to working together, like this group of leaders, "permission slips" are a great way to start building trust. We adapted this exercise from the book *Daring Greatly*. This exercise is a helpful tool to identify what might get in the way of learning and practicing new ideas.[55]

We designed our very own permission slip that read:

Today, I give myself permission to: _____

As we shared our permission slips around the table, one in particular stood out.

"Be spontaneous. I want to be spontaneous."

He said it in such a way that led you to believe he wasn't spontaneous very often. *"I am NEVER spontaneous,"* he verified. The room erupted with laughter because everyone who knew him knew it was true. I thought to myself, *when was the last time I was spontaneous? When did I just let go and give myself permission to be spontaneous?* Being spontaneous is risky in business. Sometimes it can backfire or be criticized.

PERMISSION LEADS TO ACTION

Later in the morning, we talked about the differences between good and bad coaching. I've found it's helpful to

---

55 Brené Brown, *Daring Greatly: How the Courage to Be Vulnerable Transforms the Way We Live, Love, Parent, and Lead* (New York: Avery, an imprint of Penguin Random House, 2015), 20–24.

see coaching in action, especially for leaders who want to grow their coaching skills. To demonstrate, I was about to ask for a brave volunteer to join me at the front of the room for a live coaching demo, but before I could get the question out of my mouth, a participant raised his hand and jumped up.

Not just any participant, but the leader who shared he wanted to permit himself to be spontaneous! As he walked up, he said out loud:

"I allowed myself to be spontaneous, and here it is!"

I beamed with pride as he modeled for all the leaders in the room permission in action. Well done!

For ten minutes we had a robust coaching conversation that unleashed his thinking. He was ready to take action on the challenge he had been facing. High five for him!

LIVING OUT MY OWN SPONTANEITY

It's one thing to encourage another leader to be spontaneous and experiment, but it's another to do it yourself. Recently, I was preparing for a talk at a large conference. I realized that to live out this mantra, I had to try something new. So, I researched an improv exercise to reinforce the importance of straight talk. I had never done this before. Moments before I took the stage, as the seats were filling up, I started to think to myself, *there's no way I can pull this off. The stakes are too high!*

But I took a deep breath and told myself, *one small brave move, you can do this.*

The small brave move was introducing this new exercise I was doubting. I knew telling the audience we were doing it meant, well, we were doing it. I rolled with it.

I did it. I pulled it off. The volunteers who joined me for the improv piece were exceptional, and the activity drove home an important point. It was a win! What if I hadn't given myself permission do that? I wouldn't have experienced something better. Oh, it was so much better!

I know my batting rate won't be 100 percent, but what if it was 70/30 or even 60/40?

Here's to giving ourselves permission to do so much more.

EMERGING OR FIRST TIME LEADERS

Are leaders born or made? A study of leaders indicated 52.4 percent felt leaders are made, and an additional 28.5 percent felt they were equally born and made.[56]

Taking the mindsets, behaviors, and habits of brave leaders and intentionally growing them, experimenting with them,

---

56 William Gentry, Jennifer J. Deal, Sarah Stawiski, and Marian Ruderman, "Are Leaders Born or Made?" *Center for Creative Leadership*, March 2012.

and finding your voice is key. You must get back up every time you fall. Build the culture around you intentionally, and don't leave it to chance.

Leena Nair is the chief human resources officer (CHRO) at Unilever, a role she has held since March 2016. Leena was also the first woman appointed on the Unilever South Asia Leadership team. Her personal purpose is, "To ignite the human spark to build a better business and a better world." As the CHRO, she champions having the right people in the right roles with the right capabilities and mindset, and sees the young talent pipeline at Unilever as one of the most important strategic assets. She shares in an interview with Vasundhara Sawhney some words of wisdom:

"Be braver earlier. It is so important to find your personal purpose. Keep asking yourself, 'What am I truly passionate about?' and use it as your personal compass. Remember that there is no such thing as the perfect job. You have to look at each job and ask yourself, 'What are the elements that I love?'—find those elements and dial them up. Learn how you can have a big impact in those areas. Of course, there will be areas you like a little less. But be brave in how you construct your job so that the areas that fulfill you are aligned with where you can have the biggest impact."[57]

Leadership is the willingness to move in a different direction than others. If we want to lead, then the real question, for you and me, is how can we resist the pull of conformity and

---

57 Vasundhara Sawhney, "How to Be Brave in Uncertain Times," *Harvard Business Review,* July 15, 2020.

stand bravely? How can we live the values that make us, our teams, and our peers trustworthy?

1. The first step is to have clear, strong, and committed values—your own values. Look at the work you did in the third chapter. What do you believe in? How resolutely are you willing to stand behind those beliefs? Are you willing to be vulnerable? To be embarrassed? To be disliked? To be fired? Brave, powerful, trustworthy leaders answer yes to all those questions.

2. The next step is to want to see what is going on around you. Can you see it for what it is? The *how* is just as important as the *what,* as Dean Hollis, president of Conagra Frozen Foods, told us back when we were undergoing massive transformation.

3. Finally, you need bravery to act when something is going on that is out of sync with your values. You need to say something, talk straight, or stand up to power if that's what it takes. You also need to do it skillfully, with bravery and grace, so you are more likely not only to succeed, but also to preserve the relationships around you where possible.

ESTABLISHED LEADERS

As an established leader, I know I don't get it right all of the time. I try. I fail. I try again. What I do know is investing time in small brave moves to lead yourself and others pays off significantly. I was invited to meet with a CEO of a 1.8-billion-dollar company who had been so focused on building the technical side of his business for the past several years, he looked around and quickly realized he hadn't invested any time or energy in building the leadership side of his business. It was going to require him to make many small brave moves to get the right people leading the right areas and doing the right things.

We must be actively working on all of the mindsets, behaviors, and habits outlined in this book.

"The brave man is not he who does not feel afraid, but he who conquers that fear. And how do we conquer fear? By being sure in who we are, what we're doing and why. This is what you draw on to find and harness your courage."

—NELSON MANDELA

Molly Q. Ford, VP of the Global Equality Programs at Salesforce, was invited to speak to a recent chief diversity officer roundtable I was co-hosting. She shared the concept of Allyship.

Allyship is all about moving in intentional ways. It's echoing someone else's point in a business meeting who may have been spoken over. It's calling out someone's racist joke or inappropriate use of the word "gay." It's doing the deeply personal work of educating myself on history and injustice. It is standing up for all rights and it is having a voice. It's a lifelong quest to make every company I'm a part of and build all of my relationships to be more socially aware and equitable for all.

- It is a lifelong process of building relationships based on trust, consistency, and accountability with marginalized individuals and/or groups of people.
- It is not self-defined; work and efforts must be recognized by those you are seeking to ally with.
- It is an opportunity to grow and learn about ourselves, while building confidence in others.

As leaders aspiring to be brave in the moves we make in the diversity, equity, social justice, and inclusion areas, it is important we:

- Ask
- Listen
- Show Up
- Speak Up

Allyship sits under the small actions of everyday encounters. It takes small brave moves to ask, to listen, to show up, and finally to speak up.

Bravery is a muscle you have to keep exercising, so do something new all the time. If you know how to swim, it doesn't matter how deep the water is.

HOW LONG DOES IT REALLY TAKE TO BUILD A NEW HABIT?

A myth is it takes twenty-one days, but it really depends on the behavior, the person, and the circumstances. Phillippa Lally is a health psychology researcher at University College London. In a study published in the *European Journal of*

Social Psychology, Lally and her research team decided to figure out just how long it actually takes to form a habit. The study examined the habits of ninety-six people over a twelve-week period. Each person chose one new habit for the twelve weeks and reported each day on whether or not they did the behavior and how automatic the behavior felt.

On average, it takes more than two months before a new behavior becomes automatic, sixty-six days to be exact. How long it takes a new habit to form can vary widely depending on the behavior, the person, and the circumstances. In Lally's study, it took anywhere from eighteen days to 254 days for people to form a new habit.[58]

BECOMING BRAVER FROM OTHER BRAVE LEADERS

Martin Luther King Jr. says, "The ultimate measure of a man is not where he stands in moments of comfort, but where he stands at times of challenge and controversy."

Winston Churchill says, "Courage is what it takes to stand up and speak; courage is also what it takes to sit down and listen."

Walt Disney says, "Courage is the main quality of leadership, no matter where it is exercised and usually it implies some *risk, especially in new undertakings.*"

---

58   Phillippa Lally, et al, "How Are Habits Formed: Modeling Habit Formation in the Real World," Wiley Online Library (John Wiley & Sons, Ltd, July 16, 2009).

Finally, Simon Sinek says, "The courage of leadership is giving others the chance to succeed even though you bear the responsibility for getting things done."

Bravery + Leadership creates a competitive advance, and it takes small brave moves to get there.

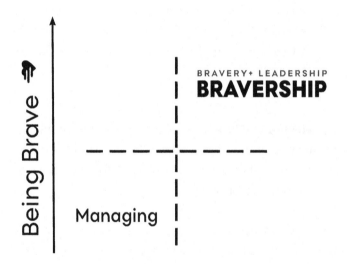

Take a moment and reflect on the mindsets, behaviors, and habits of brave leaders. What could you use more of? What do you need less of? What is just right at this moment in time?

	More Of	Less Of	Just Right
My Authentic Self			
Talk Straight			
Slips, Trips and Falls			
Lean on Your Circle			
Be There for Others			
Being Intentional			
Relentless Curiosity			
Hope Driven			

To be braver and make the small brave moves, ask yourself:

What do I need to let go of?

_____

_____

_____

What do I need to take on?

_____

_____

_____

What do I need to move on?

_____

_____

_____

14.

HOW DO YOU WANT
TO BE REMEMBERED?

———

"The legacy you leave is the life you lead."

—KOUZE AND POSNER

In 2014, I spent the month of October caring for my mom in hospice and saying our final goodbyes. She was very intentional about the legacy she wanted to leave and not only said it, but also showed us in every move she made.

On day sixteen of hospice care, my mom wanted to know the signs that would signal her journey would be ending. I took a deep breath and walked through the checklist hospice had shared with us. Just as I finished, my mom said, "Shit, I have almost all of those." Her response made me cry and laugh at the very same time. We shifted to a much deeper discussion.

She shared she had been reflecting on "knowing" versus "not knowing" when your journey is going to end. We reflected about Uncle Butch, who was killed immediately from his tractor overturning on him in a snowstorm. He never got to say goodbye; we never got to say goodbye.

The upside of "knowing" allowed my mom to travel earlier that year for three to four weeks at a time. The trips were an opportunity to say goodbye because she knew they would be her last. Most people don't know how much they mean to someone until after they are gone, it is just too late, "But not for me," my mom said. She had the opportunity to connect so deeply with friends and family, letting them know how important they were to her and hearing them tell her how important she was to them.

Losing her inspired me to closely examine my legacy and my intention. It inspired me to move *deeper* into what my purpose is, what values are most important to me, and how I want to live those. It also made me more aware of legacies being developed around me.

LEGACY IN THE MAKING

Recently, I saw Phil Collins live in concert. He has suffered some severe health issues over the past several years, and yet there he was back out on tour. I was amazed when he announced his drummer was his eighteen-year-old son, Nicholas Collins. I was thinking, at that moment, *what does he want his legacy to be? Could he be doing this tour intentionally as a part of his legacy not only for his fans, but for his son as well?* Phil could no longer play the drums due to his health challenges, yet years ago had begun to teach and transfer this gift to his son.

Then I saw this moment on stage.

They had moved over to the piano for Nic to play and for Phil to sing one of his earlier songs, which happened to be a favorite of Nic's. Seated side by side on the piano bench, Phil sang as Nic played the piano, looking at his dad with deep love and admiration. My heart was racing, and tears streamed down my face. This moment filled the room. You could feel the audience responding to the love of a father and son. We, the audience, were witnessing a legacy in the making.

"By asking ourselves how we want to be remembered, we plant the seeds for living our lives as if we matter. By living each day as if we matter, we offer up our own unique legacy, and we make the world we inhabit a better place than we found it."

—KOUZES AND POSNER

In a conversation with Barry Posner, co-author of *Leadership Challenge* and *A Leader's Legacy*, I asked him how he wanted to be remembered, what legacy did he intend to leave? He said, "That I helped liberate the leader within people."

He is not only liberating the leaders within people but also his grandchildren. At the young ages of seven and four, they are having conversations about how they treat each other and others. Posner is making a difference in young emerging leaders to experienced leaders through his work, which is a legacy in the making.

Posner shared, "I understand the way I live today will be my legacy. When I work with leaders in our workshops, we do an exercise where I ask them to imagine five to ten years from now, what do they hope people will say about them? Then I prompt them to start thinking about what they want to start doing now based on that."

As I was listening to Posner share his thoughts on the importance of legacy, I realized thinking about your legacy helps raise awareness to what needs to happen today and in the future.

"What wisdom would we impart to the world if we knew it was our last chance?" Randy Pausch wrote in his book *The Last Lecture. "If we had to vanish tomorrow, what would we want as our legacy?"*[59]

Randy Pausch delivered his "last lecture" at Carnegie Mellon University as he prepared to focus on his diagnosis of pancreatic cancer. Pausch's lecture was so widely popular that it became a best-selling book, and he appeared in numerous interviews to expound on his thoughts on dying.

Within the context of dying, Pausch's ultimate purpose was to convey how to live an incredible and fulfilling life, as evidenced in this quote:

> *Never underestimate the importance of having fun. I'm dying and I'm having fun. I'm going to keep having fun every day, because there's no other way to play... Having fun for me is like a fish talking about the importance of water. I don't know how it is like not to have fun.*

Pausch examines this method of living by speaking from his own experience in a variety of areas: professional goals, wild dreams, romance, parenting, and even competing for big stuffed animals at fairs. Arguably, the most meaningful point Pausch made comes at the very end of his lecture when he states, "It's not about how to achieve your dreams, it's about how to lead your life. If you lead your life the right way, the karma will take care of itself, the dreams will come to you."[60]

---

59 Randy Pausch, *The Last Lecture* (New York: Hyperion, 2008), 3–5.
60 Ibid.

YOUR LEGACY DEFINED

A gift or a bequest, that is handed down, endowed, or conveyed from one person to another. It is something descendible one comes into possession of that is transmitted, inherited, or received from a predecessor.[61]

Creating a legacy plan allows you to be intentional and purposeful in proactively creating the life you want to live. It empowers you to choose your life, instead of drifting from circumstance to circumstance. It should be intentional. Not only will this propel you toward your happiness and human fulfillment, but it will serve as an example and could help others achieve their own most significant success. Creating a family culture of intentionality and purpose is the beginning of legacy succession. The key is most definitely communication, both through your actions and words.

However, you define your legacy as a parent, business owner, or philanthropist. If your story is that you chose to live your best life with intentionality and purpose, then your legacy will always live on, at the very least as a model for success. That blueprint is your legacy plan and incorporates the knowledge, values, and vision that created your life.

People want to be remembered for how they lived, not what they did at work or how much money they amassed. A striking 69 percent of survey respondents said they most want to be remembered for "the memories I've shared with my loved ones." By contrast, only 9 percent said "career success," and a puny 4 percent said "accumulated wealth." Incidentally,

---

61   "Legacy," Merriam-Webster, Merriam-Webster, Accessed March 15, 2021.

these views were pretty consistent among respondents at all income levels according to a Merrill Lynch Study done on "Leaving a Legacy: A Lasting Gift to Loved Ones."[62]

What do you want your life to stand for?

Said another way, what intrinsically drives you? Simon Sinek taught us the most successful companies and leaders have something beyond profit or product that drives them. Your "why" is linked to your passions and interests—those things that have made a difference in your life and with which you find yourself curious. Our "why" also defines how you want to impact the world, and naturally attracts others to you because you're operating from an authentic place and resonating with your true self.[63]

Now, take a moment to answer these questions using a mind map.

A mind map is a tool for the brain that captures the thinking that goes on inside your head. Mind mapping helps you think, collect knowledge, remember, and create ideas or themes. Answering these questions and building upon them will help you gain clarity on what your legacy should be.

---

62 Richard Eisenberg, "Leaving a Legacy No Matter How Much Money You Have," *Forbes*, February 9, 2019.

63 Simon Sinek, *Start with Why: How Great Leaders Inspire Everyone to Take Action* (London: Portfolio, 2009), 13.

Take time to answer these questions and add thoughts and more Post-it notes around the ideas you see beginning to evolve.

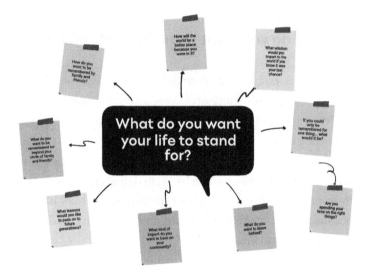

Draft a legacy statement, but just a draft.

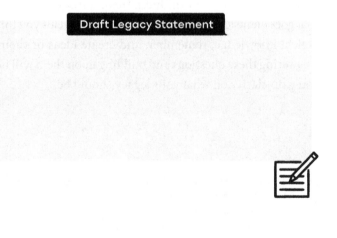

Move away from it. Then come back to it and continue to reflect and iterate.

Now, turn it into a visual. Where can you post it so you can see, read, and reflect upon it daily? Use this as a reminder to live your legacy.

Brave Leaders create a legacy by the life they lead. They work backward to make it happen.

In January of 2016, I was answering questions similar to the ones above when my thirteen-year-old, Nic, came into my office and asked what I was working on. I shared, "I am thinking about legacy, my legacy, leaders' legacies, and how important they are." He sat quietly for a bit and then said to me:

"I want to leave a legacy. I want to be known for doing things, for making a difference, for breaking records. I want to be the shark, not the sharkee."

—NIC BIANCHI

Here at the ripe age of thirteen, he was beginning to formulate his legacy.

MY LEGACY

I want to be known for inspiring bravery in my family and friends, leaders I get the privilege to work with, and my community. I want to be known for creating butterfly moments, those moments when you can feel the flutter of your heart, the flutter of change happening to transform you, me, us.

An important part of my legacy is to honor my parents' legacy. That day I found the purple butterfly in the mime's hands at the convention center set something in motion, flutters of change. A butterfly moment, a legacy in the making is a project I have founded in partnership with the Butterfly Effect and the Papillion Community Foundation to bring this national movement to Papillion, Nebraska with a social butterfly installation.

A social butterfly installation is an art project mural designed to promote positive community change. By harnessing the impact of social media and joining that energy with the contagious generosity of people throughout the world, we can bring real and lasting change that, over time, will grow into beautiful waves of philanthropy.[64] In honor of Papillion's 150th anniversary, I am leading the installation of twelve

---

64 Tasha Wahl, "Be the Change You Want to See..." Butterfly Effect, November 12, 2020.

butterflies, each signifying an important message about being the change we want to see in the world.

"Be the change you want to see in the world" with Edward Lorenz's "Butterfly Effect" theory that even the softest flutter of a wing can affect the molecules around it, setting off a chain reaction that produces major change.—Tasha Wahl[65]

The Butterfly Effect movement is built on the idea each and every person can be the change they want to see in the world by actively engaging in kindness, generosity, and creativity.

Remember my mom telling me in the final days of hospice to look for her in butterflies? Her legacy lives on in this

---

65 Ibid.

important project. My mom left each one of us children a letter we were to open when she passed away.

She ended a beautiful two-page letter with:

Now, take a deep breath and close your eyes and smile. Think happy thoughts. Don't cry. I lived my life to the fullest. Think of all of the wonderful memories we were able to make together. Stay close to your brothers. Now it's your turn to make sure you live life to your fullest. I am so proud of you and what you have done with your life. Your beautiful family. Your wonderful business. Think happy thoughts. I will always be here for you. I will always love you.

MOM

Her legacy was she wanted us to live our lives to the fullest and do it in a positive way, with happy thoughts.

"Legacies aren't the result of wishful thinking. They're the result of determined doing. We lead our lives daily. We leave our legacies daily. The people you see, the decisions you make, the actions you take—they are what tell your story."—A Leaders Legacy[66]

Your legacy is defined by all the small brave moves you make. They compound significantly and will turn your legacy into something much broader than you could ever have imagined.

You get to decide the legacy you will leave. What will you do?

---

66   James Kouzes and Barry Posner, *A Leaders Legacy* (San Francisco: John Wiley and Sons, 2006), 179.

Bravery + Leadership creates a competitive advantage, and it takes small brave moves to get there.

What's the bravest thing you need to do right now?

ACKNOWLEDGMENTS

This work was inspired by you—a leader who cares enough to lean into their work and make things better.

In 2016, I said it out loud, "Hey, I want to write a book." In December 2019, I wrote down five things I wanted to personally accomplish in 2020, and one was labeled "Write the Damn Book." Then I made a deal with myself. If I didn't write the book by the end of 2020, I had to bless and release this goal and just be done with it. Having an idea and turning it into a book is as hard as it sounds. The experience is both internally challenging and rewarding. I put the intention out there formally and my world gave me the momentum to make it happen.

On October 31, 2020, I submitted my manuscript to New Degree Press. A huge goal was accomplished. Writing this book in the middle of a pandemic was therapeutic, and it helped me practice my own bravery and learn from leaders who were trying to make small brave moves during the most difficult time in their business.

First and foremost, thank you to my husband and best friend, Dave, who patiently listened to my ideas, helped me think through how to tell my stories, and gave up countless days and evenings together for me to build this book. Thank you for being the calm to my storm. Your bravery and love touch so many lives daily. I love you so much.

A huge thank you to Jeff Shannon, my business partner, for supporting so many moments in this journey. Because of you, I play so much bigger than I would ever feel comfortable doing. Building a business that enables transformation in leaders, teams, and businesses with you has been the most rewarding experience of my career.

Thank you to my children, Moe, Joe, and Nic, for cheering me on to finish the book, for celebrating important moments, and for reminding me I can when I didn't think I could.

To my parents, Rich and Betz, thank you for showing me what small brave moves were in the lives you led. Your legacies live on. I love you and miss you so much.

Thank you to Annamarie Mann and Jen Shannon for being thought partners throughout the entire process. Your conversations helped me through the messy middle.

To all the leaders I have had the opportunity to partner with, be led by, or watch their leadership from afar, I want to say thank you for being the inspiration and foundation for Small Brave Moves.

To all my campaign contributors: You pre-ordered my books, shared my campaign page, and pushed me over my campaign goal.

Dave Bianchi, Jeff Shannon, Nic Bianchi, Rich Giese, Rob Giese, Joey Patterson, Jen Shannon, Midge Bianchi, Eric Koester, Lucas Stritt, Dean Hollis, Danielle Kirgan, Greg Harris, Deb Denbeck, Rebecca Bortolotti, Leah Vetter, Al Bolles, Pam McLean, Kristi Evon Anderson, Jodi Berck, Shannon Dill, Michelle Brown, Sue Hogle, Liz Kerrigan, Sandy Clemens, Susan Mann, Jim Arnold, Susan Henricks, Dan Hanus, Lynette Ryan, Danielle Crough, Kenton Hicks, Felicia Weaver, Jeff Branstetter, Bryon Langenfeld, Annamarie Mann, Angie Baudler, Andrea Hoig, Judi Holler, Pam Rochholz, Carrie Jensen, Michelle Krummen, Karen Altig, Carolyn Shaw, Diane Stein, Chad Armstrong, Dan Allen, Victoria Jaeger, Todd Darnold, Laurie Baedke, Steve Addison, Parker McKenna, Karen Baldwin, Debi Graham-Schroeder, Andrew Sigerson, Julie Griffin, Teresa Paulsen, James M. Prchal, Teresa Kopietz, Jessica Jones, Melissa Moore, Tammy Kielty, Lori Apgar, Allison Diesing, Gretchen Finke Patras, Tom Schulte, Russ Zeeb, Adam Weber, Connie Garro, Erika Stewart, Kate Betsworth, Hannah Lefler, Cyndi Wenninghoff, Grace Butts, Kris Myers, Denice Biocca, Dan Whalen, Jeffrey Guenin, Margie Kelley, Jennifer Krajicek, Tasha Wahl, Katrina Booker, Nicole Malone, Laura and Gerry Schwartz, Jeffrey Gassaway, Alyssa Legrand, Linda Faucher, Beth Thomas, Jill Tubbs, Greg Honey, Carole Sprunk, Steve Kane, Julie Schnepel, Christy Jaworski, Shanon Bohenkamp, Tresha Rodgers, Burke Wilson, Angie Circo, Christi Whalen, Missy Beber, Trina McCool, Richard Fires, Caroline

Johnson, Alexis Modlin, Larissa Johnson, Jodi Stice, Gordon Gunniss, Erin Miles, Chris Bouchard, Kara O'Connor, Carol Russell, Melissa Taylor, Michael Joyce, Anne Branigan, Sarah Yrokoski, Monique Farmer, Jennifer Mulholland, Curtis Johnson, Dawn Nizzi, Tony Brummels, Sharon Rasmussen, Jona Raasch, Chad Bertucci, Don Avery, Catherine Milone, Andrew Hoffner, Tiffany Seevers, Sherry Bisaillon, Robbe Peetz, Kellie Garrett, Maria Howell, Kraig Kingston, Chris Dill, Pat Bell, Tricia Robinson, Jess Havran, Catherine Cruz-Montes, Lisa Ten Kley, Gina Kwiatowski, Kevin Moe, Patrick J. Burke, Ellen Kassmeier, Linda Lovgren, Melissa Marvin, Lisa Roskens, Jessica Heinenman, Jeanne Jones, Amber Briggs, Kara Lindbergh, Kevin Pinkerton, Chris Adderton, Leslie Reimer, Kelly Schaefer, Janelle Zeleny, Tania Duggan, Neris France, Dan Hemphill, Ginny Collins, Angie Froelich, Rachel Benson, Laurie Pieper, Heather Graveline, Shirley Kawula, Amy Nelson, Dana Fries, Audrey Wichmann, Cola Svec, Dan Weber, Paula Hazen, Tyler Kopietz, Tami Bartunek, Susanne Jennings, John Laurent, Steve Oster, Tracy Crowell, Julie Clark, Donna Kush, Alison Schwanke, Alisa Parmer, Patricia Johnson, Tracy Neideg, Cara Kirsch, Courtni Kopietz, Lori Kleinschmit, Suzanne Combs Brown, Christine Karschner, Carrie Weber, Greg Honey, Percy Fields, Kori Reed, Patty O'Malley, Dave Koll, Andie Gordman, Jonie Sturek, the DeLeo's, Wing-Sze Eunise Ho, Tiz Green, Dave Hogberg, Laura Roccaforte, Kristyn Lawson, Stacia Housh, Beth Bartels, and Veronica Ploetz

You believed in me, and I thank you!

In memory of Dan Evon:

Thank you for learning I was one book away from hitting my pre-sale campaign goal and ordering my book. I never imagined you would not be here to hand the book to and hear how much I appreciate what you did.

Thank you for leaving a thumbprint on my heart.

More thank-yous!

Thank you to Michelle, Kristi, Dana, Tammy, Sue, and Jody who turned Thursday evenings at the lake into a place to celebrate each week of writing. Much of my book was born that summer and fall, so thank you for being there for me.

Thank you to Partnership 4 Kids for building brave leaders even earlier in our youth through academic support, post-secondary exploration, and career readiness. A portion of the pre-sales campaign goes back to P4K to help grow our future brave leaders.

Eric Koester, you are a game changer, and without you this would not have been possible. Thank you for pouring your heart and soul into all you do.

Thank you to the publishing team at New Degree Press: Brian, Kendra, Mateusz, David G., Kristy, John, Haley, Gjiorgiji, Jaime, and Kate. You were my guide and support and helped me make this happen. We did it!

Finally, thank you to the last leader I worked for at Markel. You forced me to play small, and had you not, I wouldn't have chased my dreams.

I want to thank every leader who aspires to be a bit braver. I see you, and I am cheering you on!

APPENDIX

INTRODUCTION

Bush, George W. "Selected Speeches President George W. Bush 2001-2008." *The White House of George W. Bush*. National Archives and Records Administration.

Denning, Tim. "Bravery Isn't Just about Being a Hero." Medium (blog), December 23, 2019. https://timdenning.medium.com/bravery-isnt-just-being-a-hero-83f9df7aae6b.

London, Simon, and Claudio Feser. "What Is leadership: Moving beyond the C-Suite." February, 2019. In *McKinsey Podcast*, MP3 Audio, 30:57. https://www.mckinsey.com/assets/dotcom/the-mckinsey-podcast/MP-Leadership-beyond-the-C-suite.mp3.

CHAPTER 1

HOW WE GOT HERE

Brown, Brené. *Daring Greatly: How the Courage to Be Vulnerable Transforms the Way We Live, Love, Parent, and Lead.* New York: Penguin Random House, 2012.

Clance, P. R., and Suzanne A. Imes. "The Imposter Phenomenon in High Achieving Women: Dynamics and Therapeutic Intervention." *Psychotherapy: Theory, Research & Practice* 15, no. 3 (1978): 241–247. https://doi.org/10.1037/h0086006.

Coyle, Daniel. *The Culture Code: The Secrets of Highly Successful Groups.* New York: Penguin Random House, 2018.

Gallup. "Record-High 25% of U.S. Workers Say Job Loss Is Likely." Gallup, April 22,2020. https://news.gallup.com/poll/308960/record-high-workers-say-job-loss-likely.aspx.

Hardy, Darren. *The Compound Effect: Jumpstart Your Income, Your Life, Your Success.* Boston: DaCapo Press, 2013.

Kounang, Nadia. "What Is the Science Behind Fear?" *CNN*, October 29, 2015. https://www.cnn.com/2015/10/29/health/science-of-fear/index.html.

Meinecke, Lonny D. "The Uncanny Fear of Loss." *Psychology Today*, April 14, 2018. https://www.psychologytoday.com/us/blog/theory-and-praxis/201804/the-uncanny-fear-loss-part-1.

Murphy, Mark. "The Big Reason Why Some People Are Terrified of Change (While Others Love It)." *Forbes*, August 14, 2016.

https://www.forbes.com/sites/markmurphy/2016/08/14/the-big-reason-why-some-people-are-terrified-of-change-while-others-love-it/?sh=3302837c2f63.

Tag, directed by Jeff Tomsic (New Line Cinema, 2018).

Vozza, Stephanie. "It's Not Just You: These Super Successful People Suffer from Imposter Syndrome." Fast Company. Fast Company, August 16, 2017. https://www.fastcompany.com/40447089/its-not-just-you-these-super-successful-people-suffer-from-imposter-syndrome.

CHAPTER 2

BRAVERSHIP PRINCIPLES: MINDSETS, BEHAVIORS, AND HABITS

Clear, James. *Atomic Habits an Easy & Proven Way to Build Good Habits & Break Bad Ones.* New York, NY: Penguin Audio, an imprint of the Penguin Random House Audio Publishing Group, 2019.

Dweck, Carol. *Mindset.* London: Robinson, an imprint of Constable & Robinson Ltd, 2017.

Gottfredson, R. "To Be a Great Leader, You Need the Right Mindset. *Harvard Business Review,* January 17, 2020. https://hbr.org/2020/01/to-be-a-great-leader-you-need-the-right-mindset.

Lewin, Kurt. *Resolving Social Conflicts: Field Theory in Social Science.* Washington, DC: American Psychological Association, 1997.

CHAPTER 3

STARTS WITH SELF, YOUR AUTHENTIC SELF

Davis, Tchiki. "Develop Authenticity: 20 Ways to Be a More Authentic Person." *Psychology Today.* April 15, 2019. https://www.psychologytoday.com/us/blog/click-here-happiness/201904/develop-authenticity-20-ways-be-more-authentic-person.

Gordon, Mara. "What's Your Purpose? Finding a Sense of Meaning in Life Is Linked to Health." *NPR*, May 25, 2019.

Ibarra, Herminia. "The Authenticity Paradox: Why Feeling like a Fake Can Be a Sign of Growth." *Harvard Business Review,* January 2015. https://hbr.org/2015/01/the-authenticity-paradox.

Johnstone, Keith. *Impro: Improvisation and the Theatre.* New York City: Routledge, 2015.

Lencioni, Patrick. *The Five Dysfunctions of a Team.* San Francisco: Jossey Bass, 2002.

CHAPTER 4

TALKING STRAIGHT—HOW SPICY DO YOU WANT IT?

Baldassarre, Leonardo, and Brian Finken. "GE's Real-Time Performance Development." *HBR*, August 12, 2015. https://hbr.org/2015/08/ges-real-time-performance-development.

Brown, Brené. *The Gifts of Imperfection: Let Go of Who You Think You're Supposed to Be and Embrace Who You Are.* Center City: Hazelden Publishing, 2010.

Scott, Kimberly. *Radical Candor: Be a Kick-Ass Boss without Losing Your Humanity.* New York: St Martin's Press, 2017.

CHAPTER 5

THE ART OF FAILING: SLIPS, TRIPS, AND FALLS

Belsky, Scott. *The Messy Middle: Finding Your Way through the Hardest and Most Crucial Part of Any Bold Venture.* New York: Penguin Random House, 2018.

Department of Labor United States Department of Labor. (n.d.). Retrieved March 15, 2021. https://www.osha.gov/topics.

CHAPTER 6

LEAN ON YOUR CIRCLE

Finding Nemo, directed by Unkrich Lee and Andrew Stanton (Beuna Vista Pictures, 2003).

Robbins, Tony. "How to Surround Yourself with Good People: A Complete Guide." tonyrobbins.com. Accessed March 5, 2021. https://www.tonyrobbins.com/stories/business-mastery/surround-yourself-with-quality-people/.

CHAPTER 7

BEING THERE FOR OTHERS

Dickinson, Emily, and Martha Dickinson Bianchi. *The Complete Poems of Emily Dickinson: With an Introduction.* Boston: Little, Brown and Company, 1927.

McLean, Pamela. *Self as Coach, Self as Leader: Developing the Best in You to Develop the Best in Others.* Hoboken: John Wiley & Sons, 2019.

Pogosyan, Marianna. "In Helping Others, You Help Yourself." *Psychology Today.* May 30, 2018. https://www.psychologytoday.com/us/blog/between-cultures/201805/in-helping-others-you-help-yourself.

CHAPTER 8

BEING INTENTIONAL

Brooks, David. "The Art of Focus." *New York Times,* June 3, 2014. https://www.nytimes.com/2014/06/03/opinion/brooks-the-art-of-focus.html.

Williamson, Mark, and Renata Saleci. Autopilot. Whitepaper.

CHAPTER 9

RELENTLESS CURIOSITY

Westfall, Chris. "See What Happens When Leaders Listen." Chief Learning Officer–CLO Media, September 27, 2018. https://www.

chieflearningofficer.com/2018/09/28/see-what-happens-when-leaders-listen/.

CHAPTER 10

EMBRACING UNCERTAINTY

Carter, Christine. "Seven Ways to Cope with Uncertainty." *Greater Good Science Center at Berkley*, July 27, 2020. https://greatergood.berkeley.edu/article/item/seven_ways_to_cope_with_uncertainty.

Godin, Seth. "The Unspoken Questions." Seth's Blog, November 5, 2020. https://seths.blog/2020/11/the-unspoken-questions/.

Schwartz, Mel. *The Possibility Principle: How Quantum Physics Can Improve the Way You Think, Live and Love*. Boulder: Sounds True, 2017.

"Stress Effects on the Body." American Psychological Association. American Psychological Association. Accessed March 5, 2021. https://www.apa.org/topics/stress/body.

White, Randal P. "Ambiguity Leadership: It's OK to Be Uncertain." *Chief Learning Officer*, March 28, 2010. https://www.chieflearningofficer.com/2010/03/28/ambiguity-leadership-its-ok-to-be-uncertain/.

CHAPTER 11

HOPE DRIVEN

Darabont, Frank. 1994. The Shawshank Redemption. United States: Columbia Pictures.

Goleman, D. *Emotional Intelligence: Why It Can Matter More Than IQ.* New York: Bloomsbury Publishing PLC, 1996.

Lopez, Shane J. *Making Hope Happen: Create the Future You Want for Yourself and Others.* New York: Atria Paperback, 2013.

Snyder, C.R. *Handbook of Hope Theory, Measures and Applications.* San Diego: Academic Press, 2000.

CHAPTER 13

HOW TO BECOME A BRAVER LEADER

Brown, Brené. *Daring Greatly: How the Courage to Be Vulnerable Transforms the Way We Live, Love, Parent, and Lead.* New York: Avery, an imprint of Penguin Random House, 2015.

Genry, William, Jennifer J. Deal, Sarah Stawiski, and Marian Ruderman. "Are Leaders Born or Made?" *Center for Creative Leadership,* March 2012. https://cclinnovation.org/wp-content/uploads/2020/03/are-leaders-born-or-made.pdf.

Lally, Phillippa, Cornelia H. M. van Jaarsveld, Henry W. W. Potts, and Jane Wardle. "How Are Habits Formed: Modelling Habit Formation in the Real World." Wiley Online Library. John

Wiley & Sons, Ltd, July 16, 2009. https://onlinelibrary.wiley.
com/doi/abs/10.1002/ejsp.674.

Sawhney, Vasundhara. "How to Be Brave in Uncertain Times."
Harvard Business Review. July 15, 2020.

CHAPTER 14

HOW DO YOU WANT TO BE REMEMBERED?

Eisenberg, Richard. "Leaving a Legacy No Matter How Much
Money You Have," *Forbes*, February 9, 2019. https://www.
forbes.com/sites/nextavenue/2019/02/08/leaving-a-legacy-no-
matter-how-much-money-you-have.

Kouzes, James, and Barry Posner. *A Leaders Legacy.* San Francisco:
John Wiley and Sons, 2006.

"Legacy," Merriam-Webster (Merriam-Webster), accessed March
15, 2021. https://www.merriam-webster.com/dictionary/legacy.

Pausch, Randy. *The Last Lecture.* New York: Hyperion, 2008.

Sinek, Simon. *Start with Why: How Great Leaders Inspire Everyone
to Take Action.* London: Portfolio, 2009.

Wahl, Tasha. "Be the Change You Want to See...," Butterfly Effect,
November 12, 2020. www.butterflyeffectbethechange.com.

·

Made in the USA
Las Vegas, NV
12 May 2021